MYSTERIES OF THE UNITED STATES

STATES

TRUE STORIES FROM US HISTORY

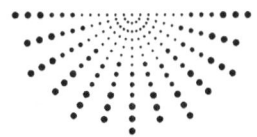

E.B. WHEELER

Rowan Ridge
Press

MYSTERIES OF THE UNITED STATES

ISBN: 978-1-960033-20-8

First printing: November 2025

Published by Rowan Ridge Press, Utah

Cover and interior design © Rowan Ridge Press

Cover image via Deposit Photos

 Formatted with Vellum

For everyone who wants to know more

NOTE FROM THE AUTHOR

The stories in this book are true, based on the most reliable sources I could find (you can see a list of the main sources for each chapter at the back of the book). Writing about history is always tricky because people record what they think happened, or what they remember or heard about, but no one has all the answers. Two people can remember the same event very differently. Even with more recent history like the mysteries in this book where some of the witnesses might still be alive, they don't always agree about what they saw or heard. Sometimes, they don't bother writing down important details because they assume "everyone knows that" or "what I think doesn't matter." Occasionally, they lie or make things up! History sleuths have to put the truth together like a puzzle, but we often don't have all the pieces or can't see how they fit. That can make historical mysteries more interesting to try to solve.

Where possible, I used first-hand accounts to reconstruct

these stories, but I sometimes had to guess exactly what people said, did, and thought based on the information available. I have done my best to be accurate, but real people are too complex to fit on a page, and I apologize if I misrepresented anyone.

I hope you enjoy trying to solve each mystery and perhaps find one that sparks your curiosity to dive deeper into the mysteries of history.

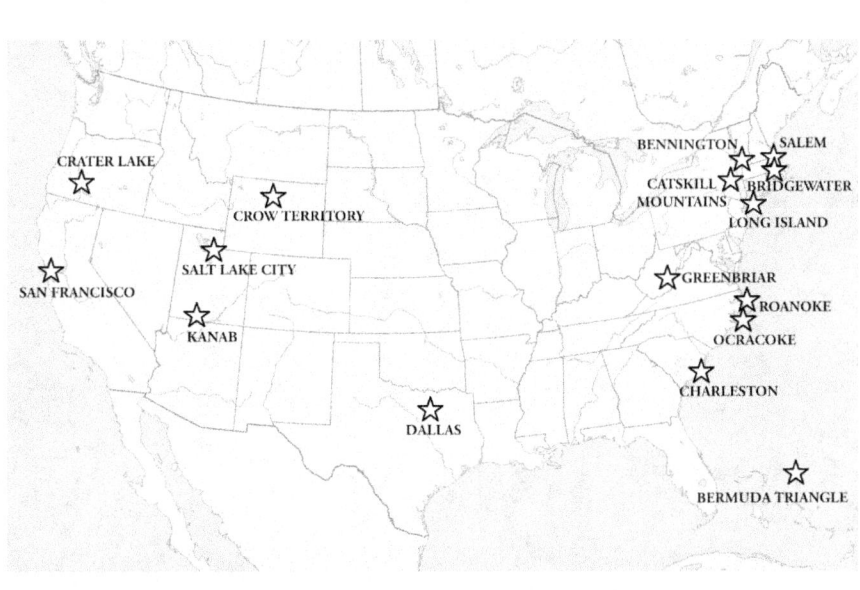

CRATER LAKE

CROW TERRITORY

BENNINGTON   SALEM

CATSKILL   BRIDGEWATER
MOUNTAINS

SALT LAKE CITY   LONG ISLAND

SAN FRANCISCO   GREENBRIAR

KANAB   ROANOKE

OCRACOKE

CHARLESTON

DALLAS

BERMUDA TRIANGLE

CHAPTER ONE

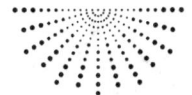

Montezuma's Gold

Kanab is a small town nestled in the desert of southern Utah, surrounded by red rock cliffs and canyons. It experienced a brief boom in the early 1900s as a backdrop for Hollywood Westerns, but most of its history has been quiet—a remote outpost on the edge of larger events and places.

Yet Kanab may hide a secret: a secret worth millions of dollars. Some say this treasure hides in a maze of caves filled with twists, turns, and deadly drops. Others claim it's in a cavern that can only be reached by swimming deep in a lake. For believers, Kanab is the home of the lost treasure of Montezuma.

Montezuma is known as the last ruler of the Aztec Empire. The Aztecs or Mexicas ruled over a vast and wealthy empire in what is today central Mexico from their city of Tenochtitlán—one of the largest and richest cities in the world by the 1500s. Though some of the people they conquered grew loyal to them, others hated the Aztecs.

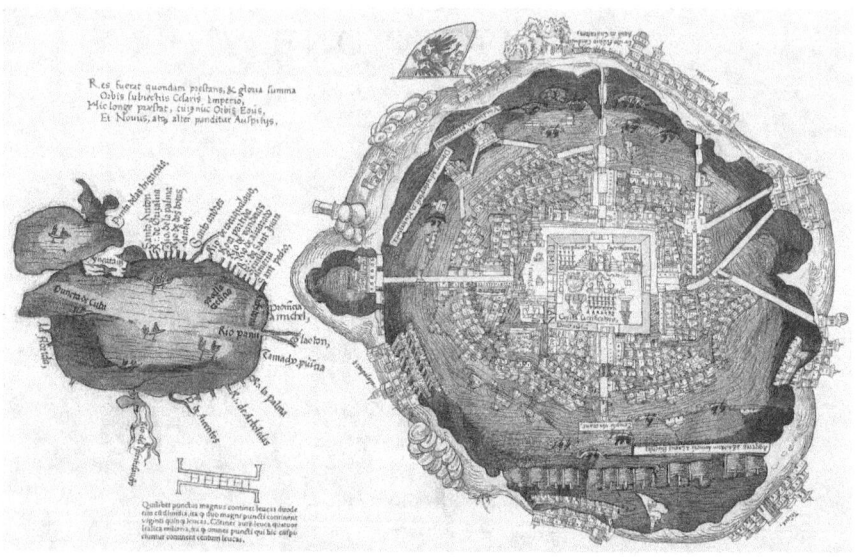

Tenochtitlan, as drawn shortly after the Spanish arrived, was a sprawling city built on Lake Texcoco in the heart of the Aztec empire. Photo courtesy of Friedrich Peypus and Wikimedia.

In 1519, the Spanish conquistador Hernán Cortés came to Mexico in search of conquest and gold. It didn't take him long to learn of Montezuma and the Aztecs. Cortez found allies among the enemies of the Aztecs and marched on Tenochtitlán. He took Montezuma captive, forced the Aztecs to bring him treasures that he melted down into gold bars, and eventually slaughtered many of the people. The people of Tenochtitlán revolted against Cortés, and Montezuma was killed, either by the Spaniards or by some of his people who felt he had betrayed them.

A sixteenth-century drawing shows Montezuma meeting with Cortez and La Malinche, the enslaved Nahua girl who helped the Spanish in their conquest. Image courtesy of Wikimedia.

In his letter to the Spanish king, Cortés wrote, "I determined to quit the city that night. I took all the gold and jewels belonging to your Majesty that could be removed..."

One of Cortés's men, Bernal Diaz del Castillo, gave more details about the night. He said, "The greater part of the treasure consisted of broad bars of gold, with which the horses and men were as heavily laden as possible."

When the horses and slaves could carry no more, Cortez allowed his soldiers to take as much as they were able so the Aztecs would not get it back.

But the Aztecs had destroyed the bridges that allowed passage over the lake and canals that surrounded Tenochtitlán.

Diaz wrote, "And before we had time to look about us, we were attacked by vast bodies of the enemy, and the whole lake was instantly covered with canoes, so that we were unable to move on any further."

The Spaniards had to cross the water to reach safety. Swimming in armor and carrying gold is not for the faint of heart, especially when under attack by enemy forces. Cortés abandoned his men and charged ahead. It was every man for himself. Many Spaniards dropped their gold in the race to escape. Diaz reported that he only took a few small gold objects, which may be why he survived. Many of those who clung to their treasure died for it. They learned too late that you can't take it with you.

Drawings from the sixteenth-century Florentine Codex showing Spanish soldiers fleeing from Aztec warriors. Image courtesy of the Library of Congress and Wikimedia.

Cortés later returned to Tenochtitlán to conquer it, but by the time he did, the gold was gone. The Aztecs, it seemed, had collected all that remained of "Montezuma's treasure" and hidden it away somewhere.

Besides the Spanish and Mexican accounts of the treasure, we have physical proof of the story of the lost wealth. A gold bar discovered in 1981 by workers under the streets of Mexico City (built over Tenochtitlán) matched the description and chemical analysis of the gold bars Cortés created by melting down Mexican treasures. The bar was found on the route the Spanish took to escape.

That was only one gold bar, though, probably dropped by the fleeing Spanish. Where is the rest of the treasure, and why do people think it ended up in Kanab, Utah?

Kanab is far from the Aztec capital. Map based on an image by Kaldari and Halava CC 3.0, cropped with locations added.

The Aztecs were not native to the area of Tenochtitlán. They had come to central Mexico seeking a new home from somewhere farther north, a place called Aztlán—either northern Mexico or the Southwestern United States. Their language, Nahuatl, is related to the languages of the Hopi of Arizona, the Utes of Utah and Colorado, the Shoshone of Idaho, and the Comanche of New Mexico and Texas. The

Aztec migration took place around 1300 AD. This is about the same time the Ancestral Puebloan (Anasazi) people suddenly abandoned their cliff dwellings in the American Southwest. Both groups were probably affected by the same problems of drought, increased fighting over resources, and other unknown pressures that historians are still trying to understand.

Abandoned Ancestral Puebloan cliff dwellings in the US Southwest. Photo courtesy of Deposit Photos.

It isn't just language and regional troubles that connect the history of Mexico and the American Southwest. Before the arrival of Europeans, the Native nations had developed complex trade networks. Copper bells from Mexico were traded in the Southwestern pueblos. Parrot feathers from Mexico have been found in the ancient settlements of the American Southwest, and the Hopi people have a clan named for parrots despite the fact that parrots are not found in Arizona. Evidence of some beliefs, like that of a serpent god, are found from Mexico through the Southwest and even to the people around the Mississippi River region—where the people also built pyramids. These things suggest that Aztec or Mexican influence reached far outside central Mexico.

Many people believe the Aztecs tried to return their treasures to Aztlán to protect them from the Spanish. This leaves many possible hiding places for the treasure, though, since we only know that Aztlán was somewhere north of Tenochtitlán.

These Aztec ear decorations are clay plated with gold, so they wouldn't have been melted down and hidden with the solid gold objects. They might give a clue about the kinds of items that were lost in the Spanish conquest, or maybe Aztec treasures still waiting to be found. Photo courtesy of madman2001 and Wikimedia, GNU license.

Some treasure hunters claim that in the early 1900s, a prospector named Freddy Crystal was looking through the records of an old monastery in Mexico for clues about where to find treasure. He found ancient documents from the time of Cortez. He had prospected in various parts of the Southwestern United States, and as he studied one of the maps, it reminded him of the area around Kanab. This, he thought, was a map to Aztlán.

Crystal hurried back to Kanab and began his hunt for a cavern that matched the descriptions on the map. It took him several years, but eventually he found a cave that contained petroglyphs and steps carved into the stone. The area around Kanab had been on the outskirts of the Ancestral Puebloan (Anasazi) culture, so some old cliff dwellings and other ruins remain in the area, but he believed these remnants were Aztec.

He apparently convinced some of the townsfolk as well. Kanab was a small, struggling settlement at the time—it didn't even have electricity—and people were excited for the chance to get rich. Local legends claim that one part of the caves had been blocked off. The treasure hunters broke through and found a network of caverns, including what seemed to be booby traps to deter intruders. After several years of hunting, no one found any treasure, only a few old mule bones. Most people lost interest in the hunt and had crops and livestock that needed to be tended. Freddy Crystal disappeared from town, though some locals say he was found with his throat cut and his treasure maps stolen.

It's difficult to say how much of Freddy Crystal's story is true. Kanab didn't have a newspaper at the time to report his activities, and he doesn't show up in any official records, including the US census of 1920. That doesn't mean he didn't exist, since official records sometimes missed people— especially if they moved around a lot or didn't want to be found. There were far fewer records of everyday activities 100 years ago, when there was no internet or cell phones, and even radios and cameras were rare. The stories of Freddy Crystal and his cave have been handed down as oral tradition—stories that can change a little with each telling, especially over many years.

Between 1915 and 1922, an archaeologist named Neil Judd excavated some of the canyons and caves near Kanab and found many Ancestral Puebloan artifacts. Then in 1920, Jesse L. Nusbaum discovered mummies in the area that were much older, from about 200 AD. Nothing they found ties directly to the Aztecs, but it does show that the area has been inhabited for a very long time. Freddy Crystal could have been working in the area at the same time as these archaeologists—maybe even drawn to the region by their finds (if the story of the Mexican map is exaggerated)—or perhaps his story evolved from the expeditions of one or both of these archaeologists.

Neil. M. Judd with his findings from the Kanab area. Photo courtesy of the Library of Congress.

Treasure hunters have not given up on the idea that southern Utah is Aztlán. Recent interest has shifted to Three

Lakes, a deep pond just outside Kanab near where archaeologist Neil Judd found some of his ancient artifacts. Some gold seekers think petroglyphs in the nearby rocks mean treasure is hidden there.

The Child family bought the property around Three Lakes in the 1980s and began exploring the 35-foot-deep pond. They found a tunnel leading off from the bottom of the pond and speculated that this could be a water trap hiding the treasure. In a water trap, the water that flows into a pond or lake is dammed, and a tunnel is dug that goes up to a cavern above the water level. The treasure is hidden in this cavern. Then the pond is filled, and the only way to get to the treasure would be to swim to the bottom of the lake and up the tunnel. For extra security, local legend says the Aztecs who buried the treasure killed each other at the site to keep it a secret and so their spirits could guard it forever. (The legend doesn't explain how anyone would know this if all of the people present were killed.)

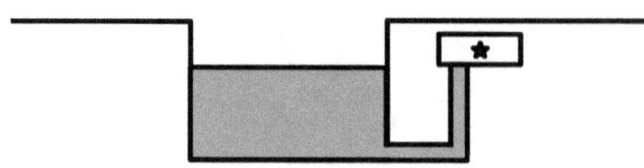

A water trap would make a treasure hard to reach.

The divers the Childs brought in to explore the pond

couldn't make it through the tunnel to see what—if anything—lies at the end. Some divers said it felt like their air was being cut off when they tried to swim up the tunnel, and one said they saw shadowy figures deep under the water. They refused to explore any further.

The Child family then hired someone to drill where they believed the treasure chamber would be. In the initial drilling, they found what appeared to be flakes of gold on the drill bit. Before the driller could come back with a larger drill, though, he had a heart attack and died.

The family next decided to drain the lake, but that plan didn't get very far. They first met resistance from Kanab residents who worried about how damming and draining the lake would affect the town's water supply. Then the Fish and Wildlife Service stopped the draining because they discovered that the pond is one of the only places in the world where the endangered Kanab ambersnail lives. Some people saw a resemblance between the snails and Aztec gold jewelry modeled to look like snail shells. They wondered if the snails were another guardian sent by the Aztecs.

It isn't hard to see why the Childs started to wonder if the treasure was cursed. They decided that Aztec spirits still guarded the treasure, and they weren't meant to retrieve it. They sold the land to Best Friends Animal Sanctuary.

If there's any treasure in the lake, it's now protected not only by Aztec ghosts and endangered snails, but also by the dogs and other animals that make Best Friends Animal Sanctuary their home. You can visit the animal sanctuary—and even see a small Puebloan ruin on the property—but treasure hunting is not allowed. Maybe the gold is down there in that tunnel. Maybe it's still lost in Freddy Crystal's caves. Maybe Kanab was a false lead, and Aztlán is somewhere else, waiting for the right time or the right person to find it. After all, the gold that the Aztecs hid from Cortés has never been rediscovered. Where would you search for it?

If you go treasure hunting, don't dig on private land without permission, bring lots of water, and watch out for curses. And if you find something historical, bring in some archaeologists to document it so we can all learn from your amazing discovery!

CHAPTER TWO

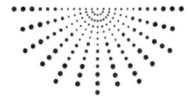

The Lost Colony

All of the people vanished. Every man, woman, and child.

John White had been gone from the English colony of Roanoke, Virginia, since 1587—three long years. He had left behind a settlement of about 115 people, including his daughter Eleanor Dare and his newborn granddaughter Virginia, the first English person born in the Americas. They intended to start the first permanent English settlement in the Americas. They hoped to gain more wealth and freedom and counter the growing Spanish influence in Florida. John White had originally come to Virginia with an earlier expedition that failed because of conflicts with the Native Americans. Yet he was so convinced that an English settlement could succeed in Virginia that he talked his family and over a hundred others into moving there in 1587.

Now they were all gone.

A picture John White drew of the Native Secoton people of North Carolina on his earlier voyage. Image courtesy of Wikimedia and the British Museum.

John White had only left the settlement to direct much-needed supplies from England. The colonists had intended to land at Chesapeake Bay, but their ship's crew refused to go farther than Roanoke Island because of bad weather. Ships bringing supplies to the colony wouldn't know where to look for them because of the change in plans, so White reluctantly returned to London in 1587 to give directions to their supply ships.

When he arrived in London, however, he learned that the Spanish Armada (fleet of ships) was launching an attack on

England. Queen Elizabeth I commanded all English ships to defend the country. When White finally found a small ship that could be excused from the defense in 1588, he set off for Virginia. French pirates attacked along the way, stealing all the supplies and wounding White in the buttocks. A defeated and humiliated White returned to England. Only in 1590 had the English gained enough advantage over the Spanish for White to arrange another trip to the colony in Virginia.

The Spanish Armada's attack on England may have doomed the Roanoke Colony. Image courtesy of Wikimedia and the Royal Museums of Greenwich.

The trip across the ocean took almost five months. On August 15th, they came within sight of Roanoke.

White reported, "We saw a great smoke rise in the isle [Roanoke] near the place where I left our colony in the year 1587, which smoke put us in good hope that some of the colony were there expecting my return out of England."

The next day, they prepared to go to Roanoke but saw the smoke from another fire on a nearer island, Croatoan. They hurried to reach that fire, thinking they might find some of the colonists. Instead, they encountered a grueling hike, no fresh water, and, White said, "no man nor sign that any had been there lately." If the fires weren't manmade, they may have been the result of severe drought and lightning.

The seas around these barrier islands are rough, and several sailors drowned the next day trying to reach Roanoke. The group pressed on, finally landing on the beach. They saw the footprints of two or three people in the sand. White assumed them to be from Native people, probably because the prints weren't made by English boots. His party hurried on and found a tree with the letters CRO carved near the top.

White had arranged a signal with the colonists: if they were able to move to the mainland, they were supposed to carve their destination on the trees and the posts of their houses so he would know where to find them. They were also supposed to carve a cross if they were in danger. White considered the letters CRO for a time, then continued on to the settlement.

"We found the houses taken down, and the place very strongly enclosed with a high pallisade of great trees...and one of the chief trees or posts at the right side of the entrance had the bark taken off, and five feet from the ground in fair capital letters was graven CROATOAN without any cross or sign of distress."

Croatoan was an odd place for the settlers to relocate. It was another island, even farther from the mainland and more exposed to storms coming in from the sea. But White had no way of knowing what had happened in the three years he'd been gone. After all, the settlers had built a fort against some threat, perhaps the Spanish or one of the Native tribes.

Inside the palisade, they discovered the colonists' heavy iron objects tossed aside and overgrown with grass and weeds, indicating they had been gone some time and had not had the time, strength, or interest to take their heavier items with them.

The sailors also found a collection of storage trunks buried by the settlers that had since been dug up and destroyed.

White recorded, "Of the same chests three were my own, and about the place many of my things [were] spoiled and broken, and my books torn from the covers, the frames of some of my pictures and maps rotten and spoiled with rain, and my armor almost eaten through with rust..."

There was no sign of the small ship White had left with the colonists.

White was distressed, but his hope lay in the carved word CROATOAN. They hadn't seen anyone on the other island when they investigated the fire, but that must be where the answers waited.

Unfortunately, another terrible storm hit that night before they could go to Croatoan Island. They lost all but one of their anchors as well as some of their fresh water. Almost out of food and water, they needed to resupply. But the fierce Atlantic winds blew them in the wrong direction—they could not make their way back to Croatoan. With their ship battered and their supplies gone, they returned to England. White was never able to arrange another trip to the Americas. He died hoping that his daughter and granddaughter were alive somewhere in Virginia.

But the settlers were never found on Croatoan or anywhere else.

Spain and England were competing to control North America. Spanish records reveal that the Spanish sent an expedition to the Chesapeake Bay region in 1588 to drive out any English settlers. They saw no sign of the Roanoke colony or any other English people except an abandoned fort from an earlier expedition.

Sir Walter Raleigh, the explorer who had sponsored White's settlement, sailed back to Virginia a couple of times after 1590, but he was more interested in searching for the mythical golden city of El Dorado or the more practical commodity of fragrant Sassafras trees than in finding the settlers.

Though he may not look intimidating by modern standards, Sir Walter Raleigh was a soldier, explorer, privateer (legal pirate), politician, and poet. He was fashionably dressed for the 1500s. Image courtesy of Wikimedia and the National Portrait Gallery.

An English exploration party went to Chesapeake Bay in 1603 to search for the lost colonists, but their captain was killed by the Native inhabitants, and the rest fled.

In 1607, twenty years after John White left the settlers on Roanoke, the English finally succeeded in establishing a Virginia colony at Jamestown in Chesapeake Bay. The Jamestown settlers heard several rumors from the Native people about the fate of the Roanoke colonists. Some local Natives told them that there were villages where the people lived and dressed like the English or where English people were held as prisoners. Others said that the English settlers had all been killed. Jamestown did send out some search parties, but the settlement had enough of its own troubles with starvation and fighting Native neighbors that they couldn't spend a lot of time looking for their lost countrymen. The English never determined what had happened to the lost colony.

What are the possibilities?

Tree ring evidence shows that the Chesapeake Bay area suffered severe drought in the years White was gone. The barrier islands, including Roanoke, are also subject to disastrous storms and hurricanes blowing in from the Atlantic Ocean. Some researchers believe that the colonists were starving and desperate and decided to return to England in the missing boat. Then, they either died at sea or ended up on some other island as an even-more-lost colony.

Other historians suggest that the Roanoke Colony came under attack by Native peoples or by the Spanish. After all, the settlers had built a large defensive palisade after White left. The Spanish claimed to have never found the colony there—and they likely would have bragged about destroying an English settlement after the embarrassment of losing their Armada to the English—but the English had a history of conflicts with the Native inhabitants.

The Native peoples understood that English explorers or settlers brought devastating diseases to their villages, and they distrusted the newcomers. Worse, when John White and the colonists had first arrived in 1587, they tried to seek revenge on the Roanoke tribe who had killed previous English explorers. They ended up attacking the wrong tribe, killing members of the friendly Croatan instead. After that bad start, it's certainly possible there was more conflict with their Native neighbors. Some Native people later claimed to have killed English settlers, though they could have said this to frighten the English colonists at Jamestown.

Many have blamed the Croatan for the destruction of the Roanoke settlement since CROATOAN (another spelling of the name) was engraved on the post. But John White didn't find any bodies, bones, or graves, and the settlers didn't leave a cross to signal they were in danger. The settlement White found had been dismantled but not destroyed (except for the plundered trunks the settlers had tried to hide). It looked like the colonists had expected to return for the rest of their possessions but never made it back.

Why go to Croatoan instead of the mainland, though? Maybe a hurricane destroyed their boat or they encountered fighting with the Native people on the mainland, and they went to Croatoan to seek help or to negotiate peace. Maybe the group split, with some going to the mainland and some staying to meet White when he returned. One of the people with the settlers may have been Manteo, a Croatan who converted to Christianity and sometimes served as a translator. He might have influenced their choice to go to Croatoan.

There is possible evidence that some of the colonists were on Croatoan either as guests or as prisoners. Shifting sea tides have changed the islands, and Croatoan is now part of Hatteras Island. In the 1700s, a European adventurer visited Hatteras. The Native people there had grey eyes—a color commonly found in England but rare in Native peoples —and said they had White ancestors. Iron artifacts, and especially chips of iron from forging, found on the island in 2025 suggest Europeans lived and worked there during the late 1500s or early 1600s. But the Roanoke colonists are not the only Europeans who came to the area. Earlier English explorers, as well as the French and the Spanish, visited the area and could have mingled with the Croatan people.

Other archaeological evidence may prove the settlers didn't move to Croatoan—or at least didn't stay there long. Researchers studying John White's map of Chesapeake Bay found small markings on the map that might show the intended location of the new settlement the colonists planned to build. These markings were covered by a little patch of paper, maybe so that if the Spanish found the map, they wouldn't realize where the English were.

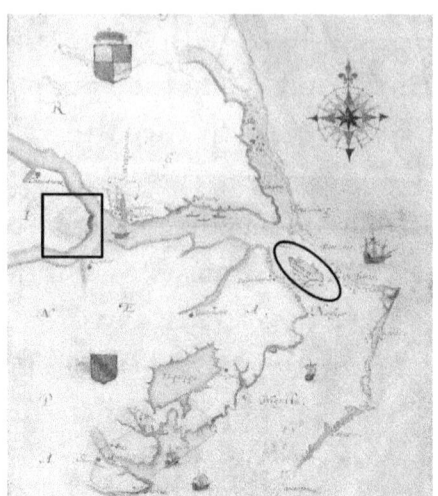

*John White's 1584 map showing the hidden spot where a
potential fort had been marked (highlighted by a square).
Roanoke Island, where they settled, is circled. Image
courtesy of the British Museum and Wikimedia.*

In 2020, archaeological digs 50 miles inland from
Roanoke along the Chowan River—on the mainland where
John White said the settlers planned to move—found pieces
of European pottery and other objects that suggest several
small groups of Europeans may have lived in the area.
Unfortunately, it's difficult to prove that the artifacts
belonged to the colonists and not different Europeans. And if
they did move inland, why did they break into small groups
instead of sticking together?

The mysterious Dare Stones provide one possible
explanation. In the late 1930s, a man claimed to find a
strange stone on the Chowan River in North Carolina while
hunting for nuts in the woods. The front of the stone read:

"Ananias Dare + Virginia went hence unto Heaven 1591.
Any Englishman shew John White Govr Via."

An image of the original Chowan River Dare Stone.
Courtesy of nasnad and Wikimedia, GNU license.

Ananias Dare was the husband of Eleanor, John White's daughter. The reverse of the stone claimed that the settlers moved inland but suffered from disease and attacks from the Native peoples until only twenty-four settlers remained. Finally, a European ship sailed past, and the Natives, perhaps fearing an English invasion, killed all but seven of the settlers, including Ananias and little Virginia Dare. The inscription claimed that the settlers were buried in a nearby hill with a stone bearing all of their names.

Not long after the Chowan River Stone discovery, a stonecutter in Georgia came forward with a series of stones he claimed to have found detailing Eleanor Dare's many exploits in America, including surviving in a cave and marrying a Native chieftain. The stonecutter was revealed to be a fraudster who often sold fake Native American artifacts. He had created the hoax stones to make money. Most historians then dismissed all of the Dare Stones as forgeries.

One of the forged "Dare Stones" for comparison to the original. Image courtesy of the Library of Congress and Wikimedia.

But the stonecutter had no connection to the first stone —the Chowan River Stone. It continues to be a source of contention among historians. Its inscriptions appear to be very old, with deep, weathered cuts that would be difficult to fake, especially with 1930s technology. Some historians think the lettering and language are correct for the 1500s and are probably real. Others say it all sounds silly and made up. The only way to settle the truth would be to find the hill along the Chowan River with the sixteenth-century burials and the stone naming the murdered settlers.

New types of DNA research have recently solved other cases of missing people, and some scientists hope that it might do the same for the lost colony. If DNA from living Hatteras Native Americans or other North Carolina tribes could be matched to DNA from the lost colonists, it would prove that the colonists joined to Croatan people. But we have no DNA from the colonists. No bones or graves from that time period have ever been discovered. If the colonists were buried on Roanoke or Croatoan, the graves may have been lost to the shifting sands and tides. If they were buried by the Chowan River, we haven't yet found their burial site. And we know so little about the other lost colonists, we can't find any of their relatives left behind in England. DNA is an amazing tool in solving mysteries and crimes, but the chances of finding this kind of evidence get smaller with every passing year.

Answers about the Roanoke settlers will probably remain a mystery unless we find their burial sites or other objects that could only belong to them. Where would you look for evidence of the lost colony's fate?

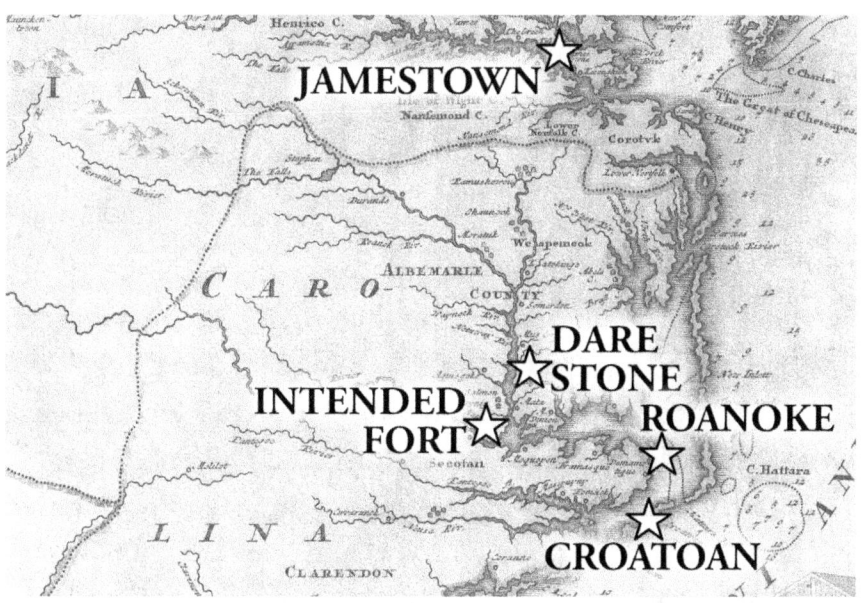

The locations related to the Roanoke Colony, based on a 1715 map of the area. Image courtesy of Wikimedia and Geographicus.

CHAPTER THREE

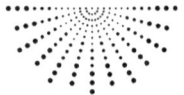

Witch Hunt

"You are a liar! I am no more a witch than you are a wizard, and if you take my life, God will give you blood to drink."

With these final words, Sarah Good was hanged as a witch near Salem Village, Massachusetts on July 19, 1682.

Sarah Good fit many stereotypes of how people imagined witches. She was a poor woman, and—as her final words show—she had a sharp tongue and wasn't afraid to use it.

Yet alongside Sarah Good, Rebecca Nurse stepped up to the gallows that day. Rebecca Nurse was a well-respected, seventy-one-year-old woman known in the village for her kindness and generosity. In fact, after many members of the community testified in her favor, the jury in the witch trial found her not guilty. Then the judge pressured them to think again, and they changed their verdict, sending Rebecca Nurse to her death.

Much more restrained than Sarah Good, Rebecca Nurse said, "I have got nobody to look to but God."

Exactly one month later, an even stranger assembly of accused witches went to the gallows. Most of these accused witches were men. One was even a minister, George Burroughs.

Standing before the gallows as he might stand before a church congregation, Burroughs began reciting, "Our Father which art in Heaven, hallowed be Thy name..."

He completed the Bible verses known as The Lord's Prayer from memory without making a single mistake.

The crowd grew silent. Some had tears in their eyes, so moving had been his recital of the familiar verses. Everyone believed that witches couldn't recite The Lord's Prayer. How could Burroughs be a witch?

Yet Burroughs had been convicted by the jury, so he died at the gallows.

In England and its colonies, witches were hanged. Image courtesy of Wikimedia.

Sometimes, the mystery in history is about *why* something happened instead of what happened. That is the case with the Salem witch trials. We know what happened:

because of the testimony of a small group of people, mostly preteen and teenage girls, nineteen men and women were hanged as witches in Salem in 1692.

These weren't the only victims of the witch trials. Another man, Giles Corey, was pressed to death under a pile of stones for refusing to speak in court. According to the law of the time, the government could seize his property if he were convicted in a trial, so he refused to speak in order to save his family's property. At least five other people died in jail during the trials, including a newborn baby. Some of those who survived jail had permanent physical and mental health problems. The villagers even killed two dogs suspected of witchcraft.

This drawing from the 1800s imagines GIles Corey's death.
Image courtesy of Wikimedia.

Why would those girls—and a jury and their community —send dozens of their neighbors to jail, and some to their deaths?

The setting for this mystery was Salem Village (now Danvers) in the newly formed Province of Massachusetts Bay. English Puritans had settled in the area to build a perfect society based on their strict view of Christianity. The English king and queen, William and Mary, however, required them to change their laws to allow freedom of religion for all Protestant Christians and voting for all males who owned property, even if they weren't Puritans.

Even before England changed their government, the community experienced tension over what their "perfect" society was supposed to look like. They hoped living a good life would keep them safe from all the dangers in their world. Science had yet to discover germs and other causes of disease, and there were few medicines. People who were sick or injured often died. Without canning or refrigeration, storing food was difficult, so if it was a bad year for crops, people starved. Faced with so many difficulties and a limited understanding of the world, many people believed that evil forces were out to get them. Having a perfect society wasn't just an important idea to them—they believed it meant the difference between survival or destruction.

It didn't help when wars with the French and Native Americans on the frontiers made people more nervous about attacks and sent refugees spilling into the more secure towns like Salem Village.

Salem Village was a rural farming community, with families living far apart and many of them struggling to survive. The people in Salem Village were known for not getting along very well. They also had trouble keeping a minister. Puritan ministers were paid by their congregations, and Salem Village had a reputation for not paying their ministers, who would then leave to find a more stable situation. So, the residents faced stress from changes in their government, changes in their religion, arguments with neighbors, bad harvests, and war.

Into this setting stepped Samuel Parris. Parris moved to

Massachusetts after a devastating hurricane destroyed his plantation in the Caribbean. He decided to become a minister to earn extra money. He moved to Salem Village in 1689 with a daughter, a wife who was said to be the most beautiful woman in the village, and several enslaved people, probably from his plantation in Barbados. As a minister, he quickly gained a reputation for being strict—even for a Puritan!—and greedy. He failed to resolve disputes between the villagers and publicly shamed them for even small mistakes. The villagers began to think the devil was working in their community.

Samuel Parris, image courtesy of Wikimedia.

The people of Salem Village decided not to pay Parris anymore at the end of 1691. At the beginning of 1692, Parris's youngest daughter, nine-year-old Betty, started acting strange. She grew vacant and forgetful, and then she had unexplained pains like she was being poked with needles, had convulsions, and made odd noises. Parris's niece, an eleven-year-old orphan named Abigail Williams, who lived with them, soon developed the same symptoms.

The pastor John Hale described the symptoms, saying, "These children were bitten and pinched by invisible agents; their arms, necks, and backs turned this way and that way, and returned back again, so as it was impossible for them to do of themselves, and beyond the power of any epileptic fits, or natural disease to effect. Sometimes they were taken dumb, their mouths stopped, their throats choked, their limbs wracked and, tormented so as might move an heart of stone, to sympathize with them..."

Another observer, Deodat Lawson, said he saw Abigail run around the room, lifting her arms like she was trying to fly, and "After that, she run to the fire, and begun to throw fire brands, about the house; and run against the back, as if she would run up chimney, and, as they said, she had attempted to go into the fire in other fits."

The girls' neighbor and friend, Ann Putnam, age twelve, soon developed similar symptoms.

At a loss for an explanation, the doctor declared it must be witchcraft.

Witchcraft at the time had a specific definition. It meant that a person had made a deal with the devil where they would serve him in exchange for power—usually power to hurt others. It was widely accepted at the time that witchcraft was possible, at least in theory. Thousands of people had been executed in Europe over the past few centuries as witches. Some of them even confessed that they were witches. Some were tortured into confessing, but others may have believed that they made bargains with the devil. By the late 1600s, though, more people began to doubt that the devil was quite so busy handing out deals. Some thought the focus on witchcraft took away from the focus on God. Witchcraft trials and executions had become less common.

When confronted with the idea of witchcraft, the girls said that two neighboring village women, Sarah Good and Sarah Osborne, and Parris's enslaved woman, Tituba, were the witches afflicting them. We don't know if they came up with these names on their own or if someone suggested it to them, something nowadays called "leading the witness."

For instance, some accounts suggest the adults might have said things like, "Tell us the name of the witch doing this to you. Is it Sarah Good?"

And the girls may have agreed.

It's also possible they came up with these names themselves based on what they observed of village life or what they had heard their parents say about their neighbors. Sarah Good was poor and outspoken, not a popular woman in Salem Village. Sarah Osborne was known for not going to church, marrying her manservant, and trying to keep control of her first husband's property instead of letting her sons have it, all of which were unusual behaviors for a woman at that time. Tituba, being an enslaved woman probably of Native Caribbean heritage, was also vulnerable to accusations.

Sarah Good and Sarah Osborne denied that they were witches. But Parris beat Tituba until she confessed that she had used some folk magic called a "witch cake" to try to protect the girls from witchcraft.

When Tituba confessed, Parris pressured her to name other witches. She did so, saying Sarah Good and Sarah Osborne were also witches, and that there were others in the village.

This led to the witch hunt mania. Other girls and even a few adult women and men joined the first girls in their fits and shouted out the names of those they believed were witches. They accused prominent men, women, and even children from the village and neighboring towns. A few of the accused confessed and named other supposed witches to protect themselves. If anyone questioned the victims or the courts or expressed doubt about all the witches suddenly appearing in their midst, they found themselves the next person accused of witchcraft. Soon, the jails were bursting with supposed witches.

Because the government had just been reorganized, regular courts weren't in session, so the governor called a special court to try the witchcraft trials. One thing this court had to decide was if it would allow "spectral evidence." Spectral evidence was when one of the victims claimed to see the witch in a vision or dream. Other "proofs" of witchcraft included confessions, owning materials that could be used in witchcraft like dolls stuck full of pins, and having unusual moles or birthmarks that were believed to be witch's marks where evil spirits drank the witch's blood. These physical proofs were much harder to come by than spectral evidence. The court decided to allow spectral evidence. This meant that if a victim claimed to have seen a vision of a person hurting them with no other proof, the jury should find the accused guilty of witchcraft.

The court began the work of trying, convicting, and hanging the accused witches. When the accused witch entered the courtroom, his or her supposed victims would scream and fall to the floor to shriek or convulse. It seemed clear to onlookers that the witches were tormenting the young people, and the jury usually found the accused witches guilty. In a few cases, like Rebecca Nurse, where the jury declared the person innocent, the person was arrested again or the jury was pressured to rethink their decision while the victims yelled and writhed on the floor at the finding of "not guilty."

A drawing from the 1800s imagines what the witch trials looked like. Image courtesy of Wikimedia.

The witch hunt fever spread like an itchy, oozy rash through the region, with so many respectable neighbors accused that people began to question the trials. The execution of George Burroughs after he recited The Lord's Prayer shook many people.

Increase Mather, an important minister and the president of Harvard (whose son Cotton supported the trials) warned, "It were better that ten suspected witches should escape than one innocent person be condemned."

Cotton Mather was an influential minister and writer who supported the witch trials. He did caution against relying only on spectral evidence, but he never expressed any regrets about the trials and executions. Image courtesy of the Library of Congress and Wikimedia.

When the court questioned the governor's wife as a witch, it went too far. The governor shut down that court and reconvened a new court that did not allow spectral evidence. When accusers had to find a confession or proof of witchcraft, most of the remaining people awaiting trial were set free or found not guilty. The governor pardoned the few who were found guilty, though it came too late for the nineteen already hanged. The Salem witch hunts were over.

But why did the witch hunts happen? How could a community turn on itself so violently?

The first thing our modern minds might suspect is that the so-called afflicted girls made it all up, perhaps to get attention or rebel against the strict Puritan lifestyle. Most

Americans today don't believe in witchcraft in the way that Puritans did, and the claims may sound ridiculous to us. We have to remember that people almost four hundred years ago viewed the world very differently than we do. In another four hundred years, people may think the things we believe today sound ridiculous, too.

In suspecting the girls of making up the claims out of boredom or rebellion, we have to remember what the judge said to Rebecca Nurse in her trial: "They [the girls] accuse you of hurting them, and if you think it is not unwillingly but by design, you must look upon them as murderers."

Were the girls murderers, intentionally sending people to their deaths? Modern studies of crime have found that it's rare for people to make false accusations about things like abuse, but it's not unheard of. Somewhere between two and ten percent of accusations may be false, which means that upward of ninety percent of accusations are likely to be true. So, which category fits the girls in Salem?

There is evidence that some of the accusers may have been lying about their symptoms. For instance, many of the people accused of witchcraft were rivals or enemies of the Parris and Putnam families. Sarah Osborne, who died in jail, was in an expensive lawsuit with the Putnams over the property she didn't want to give to her sons. Rebecca Nurse, whom the jury struggled to convict, was from a family that had a long-standing dispute over land with the Putnams.

Ann Putnam even apologized later for her role in the witch hunts, saying that she had been deluded or tricked by the devil. We don't know the details of how she was tricked —if her parents or someone else pressured her into accusing people, or if she believed at the time that witches were attacking her, only to realize later that she had been wrong. It was, however, very convenient for the Parris and Putnam families that their children were accusing their enemies of witchcraft.

Another of the accusers, twenty-year-old servant Mary Warren, started having fits and joined the other girls in accusing witches. Her employer, John Proctor, did not believe in witchcraft. He told her he would beat her if she had any more fits. She was "miraculously" healed by this threat and announced that the "afflicted" girls were faking.

The other girls quickly accused Mary Warren and John Proctor of being witches. Mary soon rejoined the other afflicted girls, once again a believer (or pretending to be), and her testimony helped send John Proctor and several others to the gallows.

Mary might simply have been very easily convinced by other people. The human mind does tend to believe what the people around us are saying, especially if we hear something over and over. Or maybe she was pretending in order to fit in and protect herself—at a very high cost. After all, accused witches who confessed and accused others were pardoned; it was only those who claimed to be innocent who were hanged.

Most of the accusers seemed to recover and move on with their lives when the trials were over. John Hale, however, reported that at least one of the girls (unnamed) continued to have "diabolical" symptoms for several years after and then died young.

The first two accusers, Betty Parris and Abigail Williams,

never took back anything they said during the witch hunts. Samuel Parris lost his job and relocated his family in the midst of the trials, so they seemed to have less to gain from the accusations than the Putnams. Betty's symptoms improved once the family moved, but Abigail's continued, and she may have been the girl who died in the next few years, when she vanished from historical records.

At least some of the girls, and especially those first ones to develop symptoms, may have had some real sickness or disorder. It's scary for anyone to be sick and not know why. It's even more frightening to believe someone has power over you—power to harm you. These girls were surrounded by people telling them witches were hurting them. If the only way to make the pain and convulsions and confusion stop was to find the person harming you, would you start calling out names?

Some of the girls might have had what is known today as conversion disorder. This occurs when a person feels so much stress that it affects their body. The symptoms can include numbness, seizures, muscle weakness or spasms, trouble with vision or hearing, tiredness and fainting, and unexplained pain. It's not "just in their heads" or "made up;" brain scans show it's a real physical reaction to overwhelming stress—such as suffering through war, government upheaval, hunger, and a community fractured by religious and social fighting. Add in a family led by someone like Samuel Parris who was very strict and quick to punish people for even small mistakes, and these young people were under incredible strain.

When a group of people is under similar extreme

pressure, it's possible for conversion disorder to spread into mass hysteria. This is especially common in younger people and in females. It's entirely possible that at least some of the girls felt real symptoms that they could not explain and believed that witchcraft was the cause.

Another suggested medical explanation is poisoning from a fungus called ergot. Ergot grows on rye, a type of grain that was common in that time and place, especially when the weather is cold and wet, as it had been that winter. Ergot poisoning can cause convulsions, hallucinations, a burning feeling, and other symptoms similar to the girls' symptoms. Yet ergot poisoning also includes severe stomach pain and hunger, which none of the girls had.

Grain infected with ergot like this can cause serious medical problems that people in the 1600s didn't understand. Image courtesy of Krzysztof Ziarnek, Kenraiz, license CC-by-SA 4.0.

Another medical problem that can cause symptoms like seizures, convulsions, hallucinations, and speech problems is a rare brain infection called anti-NMDAR encephalitis. This infection, when it does occur, usually strikes young women. In addition to the other symptoms, people who suffer from it usually become paranoid and obsessed with God or the devil. Today, it's treatable, but in the 1600s, no one would have understood it. Though the symptoms fit very well, there's one problem with it as an explanation: This infection is autoimmune, meaning it comes from the body's own immune system and is not contagious. Therefore, it could explain one person's symptoms, but not everyone's.

Without being able to interview the accusers ourselves, we will probably never know why the girls in Salem Village accused so many of witchcraft. Maybe they didn't understand it themselves. Did they really believe witches were attacking them? Were they suffering from poisoning or infection, or were their reactions rooted in fear and stress? Or could it have been a deadly combination of factors?

Maybe a more important question is whether something like this could happen again. It's easy to throw around accusations in a world where people often post their unfiltered ideas on the internet. What would you do if someone online or in your community started accusing someone else of a crime or serious mistake? What can we do to find out if accusations are true and avoid another witch hunt?

CHAPTER FOUR

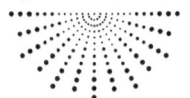

The Pirate's Missing Loot

Think of a famous pirate from history. You might remember Black Bart, Calico Jack, Henry Avery, Captain Kidd, or one of the female pirates like Anne Bonny, Grace O'Malley, or Zhang Yi Sao. But one name that probably came to mind was the notorious pirate called Blackbeard.

Blackbeard plundered ships off the east coast of the American colonies in the early 1700s. His very appearance struck terror into all who saw him. He was tall and wore a huge, black beard (hence his nickname), which he often braided. He would also place a long, slow-burning fuse in his hat to make smoke billow around him. People said he looked like the devil himself.

*This drawing from 1736 shows how Blackbeard was said
to look. Image courtesy of Wikimedia.*

Blackbeard was only active as a pirate for about two
years. This was typical for pirates, who usually died—or
occasionally retired—after a short and terrifying career.
Blackbeard was probably less murderous than many of his
fellow pirates. Some had reputations for torturing and killing

their enemies. Blackbeard seems to have relied more on his frightening appearance and boldness to make ships surrender and hand over their loot. His reputation outlived him, helping to keep him famous, or infamous, long after his death in 1718. But perhaps the most intriguing reason he remained famous is that he is rumored to have left behind a fabulous lost treasure.

Blackbeard's real name and where he came from are also a mystery. Because piracy was disreputable and illegal, most pirates used pseudonyms (false names). This protected their families from any embarrassment or legal problems from the pirate's activities. Blackbeard sometimes called himself Edward Teach or Thatch. People believed he was either from England or an Englishman born in Jamaica, which was controlled by England at the time. Some of his family, including his mother, were said to live in Jamaica.

One historian researching Jamaican history found records of an Edward Thache, son of Captain Edward Thache, both of whom were sailors. This young man was the right age to be Blackbeard, though we can't know for certain if it's him. The Thaches were well-to-do and owned property in Jamaica. Despite his family's comfortable life, young Edward Thache decided to go to sea, leaving his property to his stepmother and siblings. Maybe he craved adventure.

Wherever Blackbeard came from, he supposedly started his career in the British Royal Navy, fighting in Queen Anne's War.

This long war, from 1702 to 1713, involved Britain, France, and Spain fighting over colonies in North America. Spain controlled huge sections of the continent, including what is now Florida and the American Southwest. France held a large part of the current United States along the Mississippi River. And England had its colonies clinging to the eastern shore. All of these groups had allies and enemies among the Native people of the Americas as well, so the war was fought on land and sea.

Queen Anne commissioned privateers, or legal pirates, to fight for her against France and Spain. Image courtesy of the Scottish National Portrait Gallery and Wikimedia.

Blackbeard would have been among the British Royal Navy sailors and privateers defending the British colonies and attacking French and Spanish ships. Thanks in large part to its navy, Britain came out ahead in Queen Anne's War, gaining territory around New England in 1713 and loosening Spain's grip on Florida.

Blackbeard grew restless with the Royal Navy after the

war. Maybe he was bored, or maybe he wanted to make more money. Sailors earned money in part from the rewards that came from capturing ships in battle. Some sailors became privateers to earn more of these "prizes." Privateers are essentially legal pirates. The ruler of their home country enlists them to attack and loot ships from enemy countries. They could make good money this way, but they had to obey the monarch and only attack his or her enemies. Blackbeard may have tried this route, but he didn't stick with it.

Pride may also have lured Blackbeard into piracy. An account of the most infamous pirates, written a few years after Blackbeard's death, claimed, "tho' he [Blackbeard] had often distinguished himself for his uncommon Boldness and personal Courage [in the navy], he was never raised to any Command."

The Royal Navy often chose commanders from upper-class families. Blackbeard might not have had the right connections to become an officer or captain. Pirates cared less about who your family was and more about your abilities, so it may have seemed like a better way to make a name for himself. Pirates were the enemy of every government, but they could sail where they wanted and attack whichever ships came their way. No one paid them; they made all their money by seizing loot from other ships. Pirates could be anyone from English gentlemen to runaway enslaved men—and occasionally even women.

Blackbeard joined up with another pirate captain in 1716. When that captain was rich enough to retire in the Bahamas in 1717, Blackbeard took the helm.

It didn't take him long to capture a huge French ship and rename it *Queen Anne's Revenge*. Queen Anne had died by this point, and her German cousin, George, had become King of England. He was not very popular with the English. Maybe that was part of the reason Blackbeard turned pirate—he didn't want to sail for George I.

Thanks in part to his German upbringing, George I wasn't popular with his British subjects. Image courtesy of Wikimedia.

Regardless of his reasons, Blackbeard quickly became one of the most feared pirates. He tried a daring tactic: he brought his fleet of ships and several hundred men to South Carolina and blockaded the port city of Charleston. Anyone who wanted to come in or out of the busy port had to pass by Blackbeard and let him take what he wanted. The English colonies were designed to rely on trade with the home country of Great Britain, but if anyone in Charleston wanted to sail or get the supplies they needed, they had to pay their toll to Blackbeard.

When his men became sick, he demanded that the governor send him medicine. The governor did as he was told. Blackbeard was king of the sea and of anyone who wanted to cross it.

Blackbeard quickly became very wealthy. He had to decide how long he wanted to risk being a pirate. King George I was anxious to crack down on piracy. He offered a pardon to any pirate who would swear to give up piracy and settle down. But if they continued their piracy, he would offer others a tempting reward for their capture or death.

Blackbeard apparently decided this was the time to retire. He sailed to North Carolina (probably not trusting that the people of South Carolina would forgive him so easily). While navigating the shallow waters, the *Queen Anne's Revenge* ran aground, hitting a sandbar that trapped and eventually sank it. Those are dangerous waters, but some people think Blackbeard crashed on purpose to encourage his sailors to leave so he didn't have to share as much of his wealth. The sailors had plenty of time to get off the ship, and Blackbeard had plenty of time to load his treasure onto smaller boats and take it to North Carolina's Ocracoke Island.

He received his pardon from the governor of North Carolina and retired to Ocracoke. He married and lived like a king, leaving the pirating life behind.

Sort of.

Rumors said he still sailed his smaller boat, *Adventure*, on small pirating raids. Maybe the name of his boat is a clue about why: he couldn't seem to leave adventure alone.

North Carolina was willing to ignore his little pirating excursions, but neighboring South Carolina and Virginia were not. A Royal Navy convoy from Virginia caught Blackbeard sailing the *Adventure* and engaged in a gun battle with him.

Blackbeard boarded one of the ships that seemed to be trapped on a sandbar and abandoned by its crew. It was a trap. Sailors had been waiting below deck and rushed up to capture him once he was lured on board. A fight ensued, with swords flashing and pistols blasting, filling the air with the scent of gunpowder. Blackbeard took several gunshot wounds and as many as twenty stab wounds before a slash to the throat killed him.

The Royal Navy removed his head, beard and all, and returned with it to Virginia to claim their bounty for the death of the pirate Blackbeard.

Blackbeard was defeated, but he had one triumph over the Royal Navy: his treasure was missing. He had gathered a fortune worth perhaps millions of dollars, so where was it?

Archaeologists believe they have discovered the *Queen Anne's Revenge* off the coast of North Carolina. It holds many artifacts that tell us more about life on a pirate ship. For instance, animal bones tell us what pirates ate at sea, and pieces of a board game tell us how they passed their time when they weren't sailing. But the only treasure left on board is a little gold dust. That makes sense, though, since

Blackbeard had plenty of time to take his treasure off the ship.

Archaeologists studying the Queen Anne's Revenge
learned a lot but didn't find any gold. Image courtesy of
Flickr, Internet Archive, and Wikimedia.

The Royal Navy didn't find any treasure on the *Adventure*, but perhaps that also makes sense. Unless he had recently seized some ship's gold, Blackbeard didn't need to store it on his boat.

His home base was Ocracoke Island, and it seems likely that he would have left at least some treasure there. But where? Most pirates didn't actually bury treasure. Captain Kidd claimed to have buried gold when he was captured, hoping the promise of secret treasure would save him from execution. He died anyway, and we don't know if he actually buried any treasure. Blackbeard probably didn't. He would have been more likely to hide it somewhere he could get to it easily.

Blackbeard had married in North Carolina. We don't know his wife's name, though descendants of Mary Ormond say she was supposedly married to him for the last few months of his life. They don't mention any family tales of pirate treasure, though. Later stories of his life claim he didn't treat his wife well, though they may have been exaggerated to make for more exciting reading. Maybe he didn't trust his wife enough to share the treasure with her, or maybe she quietly kept at least some of it. Rumors said he also had a wife in London and perhaps others elsewhere around the Atlantic Ocean. If he left money with any of them, no trace of it survives.

His captured sailors said that they had asked if his wife or anyone else knew where he kept his treasure, in case he should die.

He answered, "That no Body but himself and the Devil, knew where it was."

That was a smart answer. If his men wanted to be paid, they had to keep Blackbeard alive.

What about his family in Jamaica? If he is the Edward Thache of Jamaican records, he had already given his mother and siblings his family estate. Would he have given them more money or hidden his treasure with them? It's possible, but no signs or stories of the treasure have surfaced in Jamaica.

Maybe the treasure was already spent. It's not clear what Blackbeard could have spent so much money on, but if his original treasure was gone, that might explain why he had returned to piracy.

In 2014, a man with a metal detector discovered 17th century Arabian coins in Rhode Island. Since then, treasure hunters have discovered more of these coins. New England was not trading with Arabia in the 1600s, leading people to believe that the coins are from the crew of pirate Henry

Every, who had seized a huge treasure from an Arabian ship and then returned to the Caribbean and North America. This story shows that pirate treasures may still be out there waiting to be found. Maybe even Blackbeard's.

Where would you look for Blackbeard's lost treasure?

CHAPTER FIVE

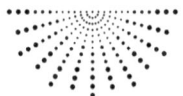

The Lady Spy

Spies play an important role in most wars, trying to learn information about the enemy without getting caught. They often use secret identities and tricky codes to avoid detection. The Revolutionary War, when the American colonies broke away from Great Britain, gives us many examples of this.

Can you decode the following message from an American spy sent in August 1779 during the Revolutionary War?

"I intend to visit 727 before long and think by the assistance of a 355 of my acquaintance, shall be able to outwit them all."

It's hard to make sense of the message without knowing what the coded numbers stand for. That was the whole point, in case a British agent found the letter. American spies had a code book that told them the meanings of the numbers:

727 - New York City
355 - Lady

All members of the American Culper Spy Ring in New York would have had a copy of this codebook. Image courtesy of the Library of Congress.

Spies have many secrets, but this message from Abraham Woodhull, one of George Washington's chief spies during the American Revolution, introduced a mystery that has intrigued people for centuries. Woodhull did manage to outwit the British officers stationed in "727" many times, and in this case, it appears he was looking for ways to sneak messages into New York City. The most interesting part of this message to many people is the code "355." Who was this lady who helped Woodhull outwit the British?

Spying has never been a safe occupation. During the American Revolution, spies were trying to find information about where each army planned to move next so their side could get an advantage. If the spies were caught, they were often executed without a trial or a chance to plead their case.

George Washington's first spy, Nathan Hale, is famous for his supposed last words, "I only regret that I have but one life to lose for my country."

An artist depicts the death of Nathan Hale in this picture. Courtesy of Yale University and Wikimedia.

The British hanged Hale in New York City on September 22, 1776. Hale was only 21 years old, and he had been caught on his very first mission. The month before, Washington's Continental Army lost the Battle of Long Island, New York. The British kept control of New York City (which at the time was the Manhattan section of the modern city) throughout the Revolutionary War and made it their headquarters.

Only a daring nighttime escape and the sudden appearance of heavy fog saved George Washington's Continental Army and America's hopes for freedom. Image courtesy of Wikimedia.

It had just been in July that representatives from the thirteen colonies had signed the Declaration of Independence, ending it with:

"And for the support of this Declaration, with a firm reliance on the protection of divine Providence, we mutually pledge to each other our Lives, our Fortunes and our sacred Honor."

Signing the Declaration of Independence was a bold act of rebellion. Image by John Trumbull courtesy of Wikimedia.

Those weren't simply pretty words. If the Revolutionary forces lost, everyone who had supported the revolt would be punished. The leaders were certain to lose their homes, their jobs, and probably their lives. Their signatures on the Declaration of Independence would become their death sentences.

Washington desperately needed information about the British army's next moves. Nathan Hale had been the only one willing to volunteer for the deadly mission to sneak back into New York City. After Hale's death, Washington still had to find people willing to spy for him.

This led to the formation of the Culper Spy Ring in 1778. This time, Washington's spies learned from Nathan Hale's mistakes. Hale had been brave, but he hadn't known much about spying. He used his real name, even carrying his Yale college diploma with him. He was a school teacher and a religious man, not used to lying or tricking people. As a tall, handsome blond man with an interesting scar on his forehead, he did not blend in. It seems he was identified by someone who knew him, and they apparently tricked him into admitting his secret mission. The arresting British officers found Hale's spy notes hidden in his shoe. They were written in Latin, which not everyone could read—but some of the British officers could. So, Nathan Hale was hanged.

The Culper Spy Ring was made up of men who knew and trusted each other completely, most of them natives of Long Island. They all used code names to hide their identities. Farmer-turned-wartime-smuggler Abraham Woodhull, the lead spy, went by Samuel Culper, which gave the group their name.

The spies took other precautions to keep themselves and their information safe, like their secret code. They also used invisible ink. If, like Hale, they were captured, the British likely wouldn't realize the letters they carried had secret messages in hidden ink on the back. And even if the British discovered how to reveal the invisible messages, they wouldn't understand them because of the code.

The exact formula for the Culper Spy Ring's invisible ink, invented by a chemist, remains a mystery. It seems that they divided two of the main ingredients used to make ink at the time, a chemical from galls on oak trees and iron sulfate powder, both in the picture above. They wrote using an acid from the oak galls. Unlike the acidic juice of lemon, which can write invisible notes that appear when heated, the gallic acid wouldn't show up until the iron was rubbed over the paper. The chemical reaction between the gallic acid and the iron formed ink and made the words appear. Image courtesy of California State Archives, Flickr, and Wikimedia.

The Culper Spy Ring was very successful. They gave the

British false information while keeping George Washington informed about the British Army's plan. They even helped uncover the treason of notorious turncoat Benedict Arnold. After the war, some of the spies revealed their identities, but many went on with their lives, never telling anyone of their wartime adventures. Woodhull's 355 has never been identified, but many women—most of them still unnamed —provided essential information to help George Washington defeat the British. Some of their stories may offer clues about 355.

For instance, two unidentified women helped unveil Benedict Arnold as a traitor. Arnold had been a hero to the American people as an army commander, but he felt he wasn't receiving enough rewards for his victories. He decided to betray the Americans by turning over the fort at West Point, New York, to the British.

Benedict Arnold is perhaps the most notorious traitor in American history because he had been an American hero. Image courtesy of NARA and Wikimedia.

The first mystery woman in this story lived at a home in Long Island, where they were forced to quarter (give free food and housing to) British officers. While the officers sat in the family's parlor or at their dining table conducting business, the women of the house might bring food and drink to the officers, take away dirty plates and cups, or tend the fire. One of the women heard John Andre, chief spy for the British, tell another British officer named John Simcoe about Arnold's plan to turn traitor.

John Simcoe was an important British officer in New York and at the center of American attempts to spy on the British. Image courtesy of the Archives of Ontario and Wikimedia.

Why would they discuss Arnold's treachery in front of this unknown woman? She was probably a servant or an enslaved woman, and they either paid no attention to her or assumed she was loyal because she worked in a house being used by the British. But she had her own loyalties, and she told what she overheard to other women in the household. A second woman in the house, possibly one Simcoe was courting, passed this information on to a female neighbor who was connected to the revolutionaries.

The revolutionaries weren't certain at first if the warning about Benedict Arnold was true, but once they grew suspicious of the interactions between Andre and Arnold, this extra evidence helped to convict Andre of spying and Arnold as a traitor. Andre was hanged, and Arnold fled America for Britain.

Women, then, had an important role to play in gathering information. But who was Woodhull's mysterious 355 who could "outwit them all?" We have several guesses, but no definite answers.

Many people believe a woman named Anna Strong worked with the Culper Spy Ring. Her husband was an American judge, Selah Strong, who was arrested in 1777 as a potential spy. A British relative was able to get him released, and he lived an outwardly quiet life while secretly aiding the Culper Spy Ring. His home at Mount Misery Head, Setauket, Long Island, near the beach, was an ideal place to signal the spies arriving by boat if it was safe to come ashore.

Mount Misery was an ideal place for contacting spies.
Image courtesy of the Library of Congress and Wikimedia.

As part of her usual chores, Anna would carry heavy baskets of damp, freshly-washed laundry down to the beach and hang them to dry in the brisk, salty sea air. Family and local tradition said that she hung the clothes in patterns to signal spy boats when and where it was safe to land. After the war, George Washington paid Selah Strong for his services to the Culper Spy Ring. Washington made no payment to Anna, but at a time when married women were not allowed to have property or money of their own, her payment may have been included with her husband's.

Anna Strong likely aided the Culper Spy Ring, but is she the woman known as 355? During the Revolution, Setauket was a sleepy village far removed from Manhattan, where the British were headquartered and where most information would be gathered. Setauket was a great place to signal spy boats, but not a great place to gather information that would help Woodhull "outwit them all." Anna was patriotic and brave, but she was working with her husband, keeping watch, sending messages, and raising five children. She may not have had time to sneak into Manhattan and spy on the British there as well.

Setauket and Mount Misery were not close to Manhattan (New York City). Oyster Bay, where John Simcoe was stationed, was between the two. Map courtesy of Wikimedia.

A woman that we know helped the Patriots at this time was a widow, Elizabeth Burgin. In July 1779, the British put a bounty of two hundred pounds on her head—a huge amount for the time. She apparently helped over 200 revolutionary soldiers escape from prison. We don't know if this happened in one massive jailbreak or if it was a slow process, or exactly how she helped them. Maybe she cleaned the prisons and left their doors unlocked. Maybe she delivered messages to coordinate escape attempts. Maybe once they escaped, she hid them in her home. We do know she worked with a courier for the Culper Spy Ring; it was his capture by the British that tipped them off to her activities.

Burgin wrote that the British discovered that, "He [the Culper courier] carried out two hundred American prisoners for me, for which reason, knowing myself guilty, did hide myself..."

She could be a woman capable of "outwitting them all." By November 1779, she had fled to Revolutionary-held New Jersey, having rescued her children from New York City but taking nothing else—not even a change of clothes (Congress eventually gave her a pension as if she were a soldier, an honor accorded to very few women during the Revolutionary War). She had been on Long Island trying to find a way to rescue her children from Manhattan at the right time to help Woodhull as his 355, though she was in hiding with a bounty on her head. Did she do one last job for the Culper Spy Ring? Or was there another clever woman helping Woodhull?

A later rumor claimed that 355 was a female spy who was a girlfriend of another American spy called Culper Junior, actually a shopkeeper named Robert Townsend. This legend said that she was arrested and held on a New York prison ship. She discovered that she was pregnant and tragically died in childbirth while in prison. While this makes a dramatic story, there is no record of any such woman captured and held as a prisoner, and especially not on one of the notorious prison ships, which were crowded, filthy, and usually reserved for male navy prisoners.

Robert Townsend

Robert Townsend kept his involvement in the Culper Spy Ring secret for the rest of his life. Only after his death did a historian discover he was "Culper Junior." His teenaged sister Sally traded letters with John Simcoe and probably spied for the Americans as well, but she wasn't in New York at the right time to be one of the mystery women in this story. Image courtesy of Raynham Hall and Wikimedia.

There is, however, another story about Townsend that might give us a clue about 355. His father held an enslaved woman named Elizabeth, or "Liss." She apparently had been stolen by none other than British officer John Simcoe of the Andre-Arnold conspiracy and taken to New York City. While spying in New York, Townsend's records show that he sometimes bought supplies for Liss, which suggests he was meeting with her. At the end of the war, when the British were retreating, Liss told Townsend she was pregnant and asked him to buy her back from the British so she would not have to leave America. Townsend was anti-slavery, but he bought Liss and arranged for her to remain with her new son (who was noted as being half Black and half White), eventually helping them both gain their freedom.

Did Liss help Townsend spy on the British? Is she the source of rumors that he had a pregnant "girlfriend" who was "arrested" by the British? It should be noted that we don't know if they had a romantic relationship or who the father of her son was; Robert Townsend never married or had any known children. If she had a relationship with the British officer Simcoe, then that might make Liss one of the women who helped uncover Benedict Arnold's plot.

The evidence suggesting Liss spied on the British is strong, but there are two points against her being 355. The first is that 355 was a friend of Woodhull, not Townsend. The second is that 355 specifically means "a lady." The Culper spies had another code number, "701," to refer to women in general. It seems unlikely that an enslaved woman would be considered a lady, a term which at this time was used for wealthy, upper-class women or the wives of important figures. For instance, George Washington's wife was sometimes called "Lady Washington."

So, we might be searching for a high society lady as Woodhull's 355—the wife or daughter of a British officer or Loyalist. While she attended parties, served tea, or even cared for wounded British soldiers, she might have gathered secrets to pass on to her American friend Abraham Woodhull.

Woodhull's family was wealthy, and his sister ran a boarding house in Manhattan used by British soldiers. This was a useful source of information for the Culper Spy Ring, but a boarding house keeper was probably still not quite a "lady."

In 1781, Woodhull married his longtime friend Mary Smith. Very little is known about her, but she came from a wealthy Long Island family. Wealthy enough to be considered a lady? We don't know. It's possible that Woodhull and Smith's relationship blossomed while they worked as spies in New York, but we have no evidence of Mary Smith's activities during the war.

Since Woodhull was strict about burning all of his correspondence and didn't speak about his spying after the war, we may never know how he outwitted the British, how his "lady" helped, or even if that particular adventure was successful. One of the downsides of being a spy is that one's work is usually secret—and for women, whether from high society or working in the kitchens, whatever their contributions were, little record remains of their activities. Now, we can only guess if any of these women associated with spying in New York during the American Revolution might have been 355, or if she was some other lady whose story is lost to history.

CHAPTER SIX

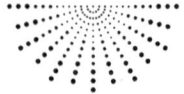

The Vanished Explorer

Imagine trekking across the North American continent, walking 8,000 miles (12,875 kilometers) over the course of two years. You have no communication with your friends or family back home. You slog across rushing rivers and over steep, rocky mountain passes. You build rough shelters to survive bitter cold nights as low as 40 degrees below zero (in both Fahrenheit and Celsius). Frostbite stings your toes. Other days, the heat of the sun beats down on your skin, and sweat makes your clothes stick to your back as your scratchy throat aches for water. Sometimes, you're so hungry that you resort to eating candles, which were made from animal fat.

Along the way, you help map a land that was unknown to your country. You hunt for food and save the lives of your companions more than once. But once you return home, they tell you you're going to live out the rest of your life in slavery. How would you feel? What would you do?

This is the story of a man known to history only as York. He traveled with the Lewis and Clark Expedition and became the first Black American to see the Pacific Ocean. But once the expedition was over and he was forced back into slavery, he disappeared from history. What became of the explorer named York?

The Lewis and Clark Expedition, at the time called the Corps of Discovery, gathered at the command of President Thomas Jefferson. Jefferson had just doubled the size of the United States with the Louisiana Purchase. This huge chunk of land had passed back and forth between Spain and France until the French ruler Napoleon decided to sell it to the United States to raise money for his European wars.

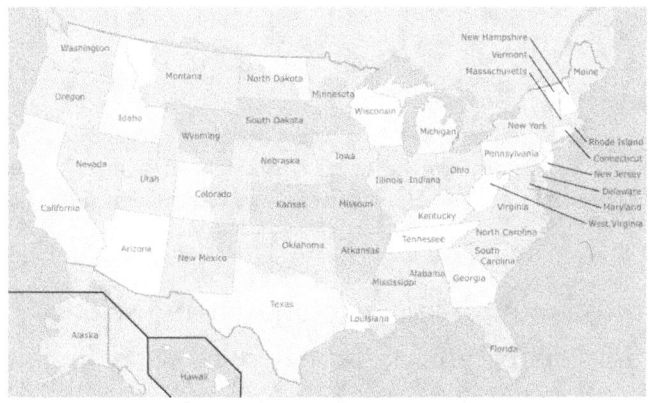

The Louisiana Purchase added a huge territory to the young United States, roughly doubling its size. Image courtesy of Ernst Schutte and Wikimedia, GNU license.

For Jefferson, it was like buying someone else's house but

not knowing what was in it. The United States didn't even have a map of the area. So, Jefferson hired Meriwether Lewis and William Clark to find a route west and create maps and reports of what they saw. They were also supposed to establish the United States' claim to the area so they didn't lose it to Britain, Russia or anyone else, maybe make a claim on the Pacific Northwest as well, and establish trade with the Native Americans who made up most of the population of the region.

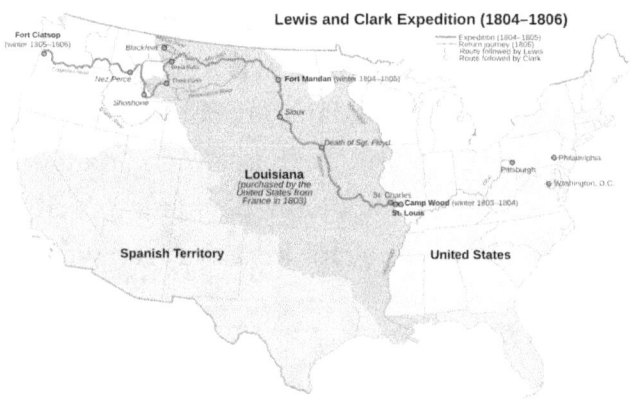

The Lewis and Clark expedition crossed the Louisiana Territory and the disputed region of the Pacific Northwest. Image courtesy of Goszei and Wikimedia, GNU license.

For those interested in exploration and science, this was an exciting opportunity. As many as 45 men joined the expedition, including soldiers and civilian scientists. Most of those going had volunteered, though they were all being paid.

Meriwether Lewis (left) was a soldier and political secretary with an interest in science, and William Clark (right) was a soldier and journal-keeper. Image courtesy of Wikimedia.

All except one. York's reason for going was very different from the others. York had been born into slavery to Clark's family, and he had grown up with Clark. In their early years, maybe they had played together, but as they grew and their different situations in life became more obvious, York turned instead into a sort of bodyguard to Clark.

We don't know if he liked Clark or not—slaves were forbidden from learning to read and write, so we don't have his opinion on the matter. Some of the other men on the expedition didn't want to travel with a Black man, and one attacked him and threw sand into his eyes at the beginning of the trip. But regardless of how York—or anyone else—felt about it, he was going West.

In fact, he was leaving behind a wife in Kentucky. He probably hoped that by being useful on the expedition, he might gain his freedom, or the money to buy his freedom, and be able to return to his wife.

The expedition started at Camp Dubois on the Wood River in Illinois in the spring of 1804. They thought they could sail along rivers all the way to the Pacific Ocean. They had no idea how wrong they were. They knew the Southwest was desert and unfriendly to travelers, but they pictured the Northwest as an easy boat ride away. They were not accounting for the massive Rocky Mountains standing in their path.

The Rocky Mountains were difficult terrain to pass.
Painting by Albert Bierstadt, courtesy of Wikimedia.

It didn't take them long to establish contact with French traders and Native Americans in the area. The Lakota Sioux were especially wary of their presence. The French traders were few in number, and the Native people didn't want more non-Natives coming into their territories, knowing it would disrupt their lives. Here, York served the party in an unexpected way. The Native people had seen White Frenchmen and Russians, but most had never seen a Black man before. Their reactions varied from thinking him interesting to being afraid of him. This made York a good person to help negotiate with the Native Americans along their journey. In one case, a Native leader later said they had planned to kill the entire Lewis and Clark party, but they were afraid to because they thought York must have some "big medicine" or strong magic.

When Lewis and Clark reached North Dakota and faced their trip into the Rocky Mountains, it became clear that they needed help to navigate their way through. Taking boats up the mountains would not be an option. This is where they enlisted the help of Sacagawea, the young wife of a French fur trapper. She had been taken captive from among the Shoshone farther west, where she had grown up, and knew several Native languages, as well as the territory in the area.

This painting of the expedition by Amon Carter shows both York and Sacagawea. Image courtesy of the Carter Museum of American Art and Wikimedia.

Bringing her along meant also bringing her newborn son and her husband, who was not much of an explorer, almost tipping over his boat and losing all the important papers. At least he was a good cook.

Maybe York felt some empathy with Sacagawea, though neither of them left a record of their feelings about the trip. It was her husband and not herself who would be paid for her work because married women did not have legal rights at this time. That did not bode well for enslaved York, who had even fewer rights.

Still, on the trip, York had freedoms that many enslaved people did not. He was allowed to use a gun and proved to be an excellent hunter, often bringing meat back to keep the party from starving. He had a vote the same as all the other expedition members (including Sacagawea) when they decided where to stay for the winter.

When the Lewis and Clark Expedition returned to the East, they were celebrated as heroes. The White men in the expedition were paid, as promised. This was what York had been waiting for—his chance to get his freedom and return to his wife in Kentucky.

But Clark wasn't interested in freeing York. He didn't pay him for his work, either. The most he would allow was hiring York out to a farmer in Kentucky near where York's wife lived.

Then the people who owned his wife sold her farther south.

York must have been devastated. Everything he had done, all the freedoms he had enjoyed on the expedition, and now he had nothing. His wife was torn from him. No one remembered him or his accomplishments. Clark wanted things to go back to exactly as they had been before the expedition. Apparently, York complained of his treatment, because Clark warned that if York tried to escape, he was to be sold to New Orleans or given to a cruel master who would beat the impulse out of him.

And that's where York disappears from the records.

Clark wrote many years later that he eventually gave York his freedom and the money to buy a wagon so he could be a freight driver. According to his account, York hated being free, struggled to succeed at business, and missed the "good old days" when he was enslaved. This was a common story that slave owners told about freed people, but it usually wasn't true. It's hard to imagine that someone who had proved so capable on the expedition across the continent would suddenly fall apart when freed. Clark claimed that York decided to return to slavery, but died of cholera before he could reach Clark.

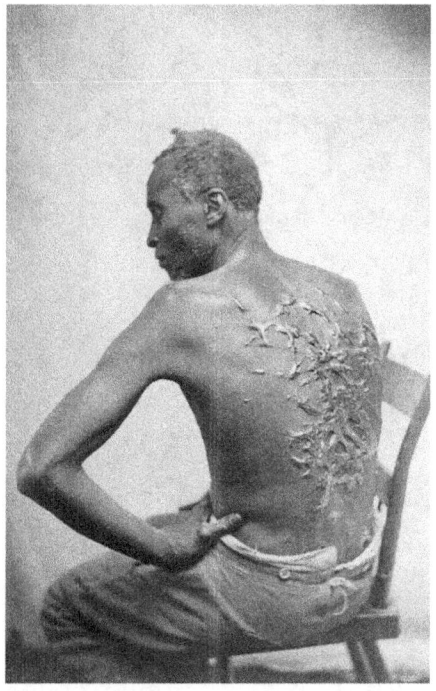

The scars on this formerly enslaved man's back are a reminder of why free Blacks were unlikely to returned to slavery. Image courtesy of Wikimedia.

Besides the unlikely behavior of a freed person begging to return to slavery, there's another hole in Clark's story. Freeing an enslaved person required paperwork, and no paperwork exists showing that Clark freed York. It's possible the paperwork was lost, but it adds another layer of doubt to Clark's story.

Yet York was no longer with Clark, so what became of the enslaved explorer?

Clark's story might have been partly true. Maybe he allowed York the unofficial freedom to run his own freighting business. Slave owners sometimes let enslaved people rent out their labor, taking a cut of their earnings. York could have been saving his portion of the money to buy his own freedom and that of his wife. It's also possible that York died of cholera. This was before germs had been discovered and people knew the importance of boiling or purifying their water, so diseases like cholera that spread through dirty water were common.

There are other possibilities, though. With the skills he gained on the expedition, it isn't hard to imagine York being able to escape from slavery and forge his own path. Clark no doubt would not want to admit that York had run away from him, so he might have made up the cholera story. Maybe York went south to find his lost wife. There's no record of him freeing her, though. If he succeeded, their happily ever after was a secret one.

A report from American fur trader Zenas Leonard offers another possible ending for York's story. Leonard reported meeting a Black man living among the Crow people in 1832 in what is now Wyoming. The Black man reportedly told

Leonard that he had first come West with Lewis and Clark. If this account is accurate, then at some point, York journeyed out West and rejoined the people who had treated him with respect, finally enjoying a life of freedom.

What do you think happened to York when he slipped away from the bands of slavery and the notice of history?

CHAPTER SEVEN

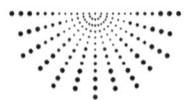

Oregon Treasure Hunt

Most US states have tales of lost treasure. In the American West, where mining was an important part of early non-Native settlement, there are numerous legends of cursed mines and hidden wealth. In fact, several states have tales of a Lost Cabin Mine or a Lost Cabin Treasure. The details vary, but most of these stories say that an old miner hid his gold under his cabin before he died—a vast fortune waiting to be found. There's probably not much left of any mining cabin after so many years, but the legends say the treasure is still out there if some sharp-eyed hiker or treasure-seeker can spot the remnants of the old miner's home.

Oregon has its own version of the Lost Cabin Mine story. Like the similar tales, we don't know who started the story or who the old miner was supposed to be, and we have no maps showing where the lost cabin might hide. Yet the Oregon Lost Cabin Mine legend has an interesting twist. We know people believed in the mine and have been looking for it since the early 1850s. The reason we know this is because those early treasure seekers discovered a different kind of treasure in the Oregon wilderness—one that half a million people come to see every year.

This Lost Cabin Mine story starts like most with a rumor. In this case, it was a rumor of a lost mine in Oregon.

In January of 1848, workers at Sutter's Mill in central California discovered gold in the South Fork American River. At the time, California was contested territory between the United States and Mexico as part of the Mexican-American War. Not many non-Native people lived in the area. But in February 1848, the war ended with a treaty that gave California and the rest of the American Southwest to the United States. News traveled slowly at the time, but by the winter of 1848, most of the world knew that gold had been discovered in the newly-acquired US territory of California.

Miners came from all over the world hoping to strike it rich.
Image courtesy of Wikimedia.

By early 1849, the California Gold Rush had begun. Hundreds of thousands of potential miners streamed into the American West from the eastern United States and all over the world.

Most of these "Forty-niners" found lots of hard work and not much gold. Many of them either returned home or turned to different jobs to make a living. But a few did strike it rich, and many more continued dreaming of gold.

Most Forty-niners found adventure but not wealth. Image courtesy of the California Historical Society and Wikimedia.

The Oregon Lost Cabin Mine story claims to tell of one of those who struck it rich. It says a miner regularly rode into the town of Yreka in northern California with gold nuggets to spend. Of course, he wouldn't tell anyone where his mine was, but he did let slip it was in Oregon. Apparently, he had a cabin there, and plenty of gold stored up in the cabin.

And then one spring, the miner suddenly stopped visiting town. A lot of things could go wrong for a miner living on his own, from sickness and accidents to attacks by Native Americans or other miners. But some of the miners from Yreka decided it was worth riding north, piecing together the clues the old miner had left, to see if they could find his cabin. If he needed help, they could help him. If he was beyond help, well, then he wouldn't care much what became of that treasure hidden under his floorboards.

This is where John Hillman enters the story and gives it a solid footing in history. Hillman and his father had come West as Forty-niners. By 1853, John Hillman was still chasing the elusive dream of gold. He hadn't struck it rich, so he made a living doing labor around Jacksonville, Oregon.

Hillman was working in town when the California miners came through on their quest for the Lost Cabin Mine. Hillman overheard their plans and decided to join the search —whether the Californians wanted him along or not. He and few friends trailed the Californians when they headed into the mountains. The two groups were wary of each other at first, but eventually decided to join forces since they had such a huge area to explore. They were venturing in the high, wooded mountains of Oregon—a place rarely visited by White men and even avoided by many of the Native inhabitants.

While searching for clues to the cabin's location, Hillman and the mule he rode came within a breath of a sudden and terrible end.

According to *Offbeat Oregon*, Hillman recounted, "Not until my mule stopped within a few feet of the rim...did I look down, and if I had been riding a blind mule I firmly believe I would have ridden over the edge to death and destruction."

Crater Lake wasn't the treasure the miners were searching for. Image courtesy of WolfmanSF and Wikimedia CC BY SA 3.0

Hillman had just discovered a jewel, though not the type he was looking for. He was the first White man to stand on the edge of Crater Lake, an ancient volcano whose caldera filled with sapphire-blue water. It's the deepest lake in America and one of the deepest in the world. It has no rivers flowing in or out, being filled only by rain and snow, and no fish lived in the pristine waters until people stocked it for fishing. It's a strange and beautiful place, sacred to the Klamath people of southern Oregon and northern California, who still tell ancestral stories about when the volcano that once occupied the site exploded and created the crater. It's a treasure of America.

Though Hillman and his companions appreciated the beauty and wonder of the place they discovered, what about the lost mine? They never found it. Hillman said, "We went back as poor as we left, for we did not find the mythical 'Lost Cabin Mine.'" Or if they did, they kept it surprisingly secret.

Even the lake remained a lost treasure for a time. Hillman's party had become so turned around in their adventure that they couldn't give anyone good directions on where to find the lake when they returned. In the 1850s, people were distracted by searching for gold and fighting the Native inhabitants. It was the next decade before anyone began to explore and study Crater Lake. But in 1902, it became one of the United States' first national parks, and the only national park in Oregon.

And the cabin? Whatever markers or landmarks supposedly pointed to the miner's treasure are lost to time. When Hillman told his account, he didn't mention which landmarks they were looking for. All we know is that the treasure would be somewhere near Crater Lake, probably in the Rogue River area of Oregon.

An Oregon lawyer and storyteller wrote about his own adventure looking for a lost mine in the Crater Lake area in 1868. According to him, a man from the East Coast came into his law offices with a letter from a cousin who had found a mine in the area around Jacksonville in 1853, but then had been mortally wounded by one of the local Rogue River tribes. The cousin apparently died in the middle of writing directions to Ted on how to find his cabin, ending with a blot on the paper. Sam Simpson thought there was enough information to try to find the lost stash of gold.

According to Simpson, he and Ted headed into the wilderness to search for the cabin. They reached the end of instructions in the letter and had almost given up hope when the ghost of the miner appeared to Simpson in a dream or vision and wrote another clue on the letter. They followed this clue until they reached the ruins of the cabin. There, beneath its floor, they discovered the vault where the gold was supposed to be stored.

Simpson claimed that Ted became so excited that he accidentally shot himself and died right there in the cabin... And the next thing Simpson knew, he was being rescued on the stagecoach road after having lost his mind and wandered lost through the wilderness, apparently driven mad by Ted's death. Some people think he might have fought with Ted over the gold and either killed him or been injured by him. Many more people doubt that Ted ever existed or that Simpson found anything in the wilderness. Simpson certainly didn't end up wealthy, and there's no historical record of a man named Ted who found a lost treasure.

Sam Simpson was known for wild tales, so it's best to not take his story too seriously. But records do show that he closed up his law offices in the summer of 1868 for some kind of trip. Maybe he really did find clues about Oregon's Lost Cabin Mine. If so, Simpson tells us that the treasure is in a hidden valley. You would find it by following a path leading off from the Old California Trail—at this point it would be very overgrown—leading to a spring and a large, notable rock. From there, you would need to find a little valley between two mountain ridges—and hopefully a helpful ghost would offer you some tips on where to look.

Some of that area is part of Crater Lake National Park, and taking a historical treasure from its lands would be illegal, since national parks belong to the entire country. The discoverer would get credit for the find, though, which would probably be put on display at the park, and possibly a nice reward, too. As long as you hike safely, you'll enjoy beautiful scenery while looking for this lost treasure. And who knows what else you might find on your adventure?

The Rogue River wilderness area. Courtesy of the Bureau of Land Management and Wikimedia.

CHAPTER EIGHT

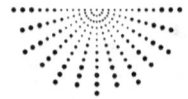

Danger in the Water

February 17, 1864 was a cold, dark night off the coast of South Carolina. The Civil War had been raging for nearly three years, ever since South Carolina and the other Southern states had seceded from the United States in an effort to protect the practice of slavery. The country was torn apart by the war, bringing suffering and death across the nation, but especially in the eastern states.

The *USS Housatonic*, a Union (Northern) ship, patrolled the waters off South Carolina as part of a blockade. The blockade prevented Confederate (Southern) states from trading their cotton and other goods with foreign countries and raising more money to support the war. The *Housatonic* had captured several blockade runners, or boats trying to get past the Union ships, and had even shot at Charleston.

The Housatonic. *Image courtesy of Wikimedia.*

The sailors of the *Housatonic* always had to be on guard, waiting for the next time the Confederates would attack or try to send a ship past the blockade. On the night of February 17th, one of the lookouts spotted what looked like a plank floating in the water toward the ship. Both sides in the war were always developing new technologies to attack the other, so the sailors were cautious of anything that looked strange. The lookout sounded the alarm.

The sailors rushed to their stations, but they were already too late to save their ship from what was coming.

The strange object in the water rammed the side of the *Housatonic*. A moment later, a huge explosion rocked the ship. The sailors ran for the lifeboats. When those were full, the remaining men climbed the rigging to stay out of the water as the ship sank. In fact, only five crew members died in the attack, but the boat was lost, dealing a blow to the Union forces.

The *Housatonic* became the first ship in history to be lost to a submarine attack.

A drawing of the fatal explosion. Image courtesy of the Library of Congress.

The submarine was the *H.L. Hunley*, a Confederate experiment. The Civil War between the North and South was one of the first modern wars, meaning a war that raced to put new technologies to use against the enemy. Better weapons were always an advantage in war, and inventions played a part in victories in the past. The stirrup allowed men on horseback to keep their balance while fighting men on the ground. Longbows that could shoot arrows with great force allowed archers to defeat horsemen in armor. Gunpowder blew holes in the walls of castles that had withstood the attacks of archers.

But modern wars use fast-changing modern technology and require quick changes in strategies. Submarines were one of these new technologies that would change warfare forever. The *Hunley* was made of iron in an age of wooden ships and powered by seven men cranking a propeller.

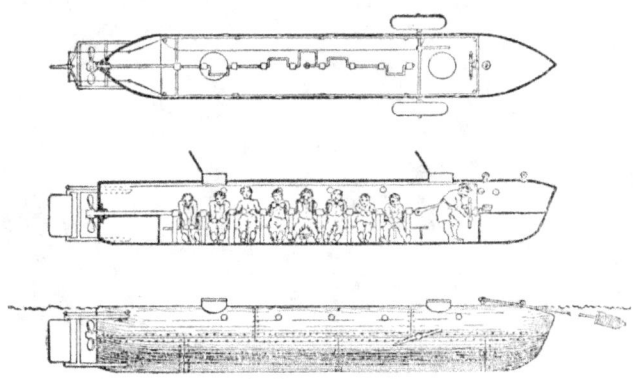

A diagram of the Hunley *showing how men would sit and crank the propeller. Image courtesy of* Popular Science Monthly.

So, did the *Hunley* go on to strike terror into the hearts of Union sailors?

It did not. In fact, after that first successful attack, it sailed into mystery. The *Hunley* vanished beneath the waters. Confederate lookouts reported seeing the blue light that marked the *Hunley*'s successful mission, and a Union sailor clinging to the *Housatonic* also saw the blue light. But the submarine never returned to base. The vessel and its eight crew members vanished beneath the waves.

In 1995, underwater archaeologists uncovered the wreckage of the *Hunley* in the sands of the ocean floor. In 2000, scientists raised the vessel. This has only intensified the debate about what brought about the sinking of the world's first successful attack submarine.

Scientists studying the wreckage of the Hunley. *Image courtesy of the US Navy and Wikimedia.*

The bodies of all eight crew members were found still sitting at their stations. There was no sign they had panicked, such as if the sub had begun taking on water. Researchers have found no obvious damage or other reason that the sub sank instead of returning to base.

The *Hunley* was an experiment created by Confederate engineer Horace L. Hunley. It had struggled from the beginning with problems. Before its successful mission, it had sunk twice, killing some or all of the men on board, including its inventor.

The first sinking occurred at the dock. It's unclear exactly what caused the sinking. Survivors said water rushed into the open sub hatch, either from the wake of a passing ship or because another ship's ropes became entangled with it and pulled it on its side. Three of the eight crew escaped, but the other five drowned. It took a week to drag the sub back up and empty it out.

Horace Hunley wanted to prove the sub was safe, so he led the next expedition along with seven other crew members. The *Hunley* sailed off and went beneath the water. After a long wait, it became obvious the "fish boat" was lost once again. This time, all eight crew members died. The Confederate Navy found the *Hunley* with one of the valves open and the wrench to close the valve on the floor. Maybe Hunley forgot to close the valve, or maybe he was trying to close it, dropped the wrench, panicked, and was unable to shut out the sea before it sucked the sub down. It was clear the crew had been trying to return to the surface—they had been loosening the weights that held the sub underwater when they drowned.

It's impressive that anyone was willing to try the sub again. Maybe the new crew members felt that the other disasters had been human error and they could do better. Maybe they were desperate to break the Union blockade. Maybe they just thought that "the third time's the charm."

Would you have been willing to ride in the Hunley? *Image courtesy of the US Naval Historical Center and Wikimedia.*

In the *Hunley's* third and final sinking, it doesn't look like human error was the problem. The bones of the crew members were found at their stations, and none of the skeletons showed serious damage (any small injuries to their flesh would have been long gone since only bones remained).

The sub wasn't where anyone expected, which was part of the reason it had taken so long for anyone to find the wreckage. They thought it would have been returning to shore, but instead it was found about half a mile farther out to sea, past the wreckage of the *Housatonic*. One of the hatches was locked, meaning no one had tried to escape the ship through it. The other was unlocked but would have stayed sealed shut as long as the sub stayed upright. All the portholes that could allow light in were closed, which means no one could see the ship, and the ship couldn't see out. The pumps were not working to pump water out, which one would expect if water had leaked into the boat.

There are several theories about what happened to the Hunley.

One idea is that the explosion that sank the *Housatonic* was so powerful that the shockwave instantly killed the men at their posts in the *Hunley*. The submarine then drifted out to sea and sank. The explosion was a huge one. The *Hunley's* charge contained 135 pounds of gunpowder, and the submarine was only 16 feet from the charge when it touched the *Housatonic* and went off. The men in the submarine were trapped in a tiny metal tube in range of the shockwaves. Shockwaves from bombs have been proven to kill people in war. Scientists have run experiments showing that it's possible that the shockwaves from the explosion would have killed the men. But other experiments have suggested that the men could have survived the blast.

The strongest argument against this theory is that several people saw the *Hunley*'s blue light signal after the blast, suggesting that the crew of the *Hunley* survived the initial blast. For the shockwave theory to be correct, the various witnesses who saw the blue light must have mistaken some other light for the *Hunley*'s signal.

The Union sailor who spotted the blue light said he saw the light between his own ship and the ship coming to his rescue. We're not sure why the submarine was going farther out to sea. It's possible, though, that the *Hunley*, running blind to avoid being seen by the enemy, came too close to the rescue ship. The sub had been tipped once before, probably by another ship's wake. It did have one hatch unlocked, possibly for sending the blue light signal, so if it had tipped, it might have taken on water. If so, the rescue ship unknowingly avenged the *Housatonic* by tipping and sinking the *Hunley*. But if the sub had taken on water, it must have happened very quickly, or else the men would not have remained sitting at their stations.

Still others think that the *Hunley*'s crew ran out of oxygen. They were headed away from the shore, and perhaps the tides made it difficult to make their way back. Maybe they were even disoriented in the darkness or from having been so close to the massive explosion. When people run out of oxygen, they will feel sick at first, but then they become tired, slip into sleep, and never wake up. But they didn't make it very far from the *Housatonic*. Why would they have run out of oxygen so quickly? Were they too afraid to open the hatch for fresh air with enemy ships nearby?

For now, we don't know what sank the *Hunley*. What do you think happened to the crew? What experiments might help us understand what happened to destroy the short-lived victory of the world's first successful war submarine?

This pocket watch, found in the submarine, belonged to Hunley *commander George Dixon. Image courtesy of the US Navy and Wikimedia.*

CHAPTER NINE

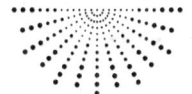

The Greenbriar Ghost

Elva Zona Heaster Shue isn't a name most people know. In fact, Zona lived a fairly quiet life, and like many people of the past, would normally be mostly forgotten. Very few names in history are remembered, but that doesn't mean those other people didn't matter. They were part of the fabric of history and helped shaped its course in small ways that add up one thread at a time.

Zona's claim to fame didn't come in her lifetime. In fact, it came because of her death. Zona's is the only known case in US history where a ghost helped to convict her own murderer.

At least, that's what her mother wanted everyone to believe.

Zona Heaster married Erasmus "Trout" Shue in October of 1896. By January 1897, she was dead. The doctor concluded that she had died of a pregnancy complication—perhaps fainting on the stairs or having a heart attack. This wasn't uncommon at the time. Germs and many aspects of the human body were only barely understood in the late 1800s. Without modern medicine, pregnancy and childbirth were dangerous times for women.

Childbirth wasn't the only thing that was dangerous for women, though. Based on laws in the 1800s, women had very few rights. They couldn't vote in most states, and they couldn't sit on juries—sometimes until the 1970s!—but that was only the beginning. In most cases, married women couldn't own property, hold onto their money or a bank account, or have any legal say about their children or their own well-being. Once they were married, the law treated them like little more than the property of their husband. It was difficult to get a divorce even if a husband was abusive. Their happiness depended on marrying someone who would treat them as a partner instead of a possession.

American women fought for many decades to have the same rights as men. Image courtesy of Wikimedia.

Of course, there were many happy marriages where the

husband and wife were loving and worked together. Trout certainly seemed to care about his wife. He sent a neighbor boy to check on Zona that fateful day, wanting to see if she needed anything while he worked in his blacksmith's shop. The boy found her lying on the floor.

As *The Monroe Watchman* reported, "The body was lying stretched out perfectly straight with feet together, one hand lying by the side and the other lying across the body, the head was slightly inclined to one side."

The boy hurried back to report that Zona appeared to be dead. Trout sent for a doctor and rushed home. By the time the doctor arrived, Trout had already cleaned and dressed his wife's body, a very unusual action for the time. Preparing bodies for burial—especially women's bodies—was work for women. It was a way for family and friends to say goodbye. But Trout took the lead and refused any help.

When the doctor confirmed that Zona was dead, Trout asked him not to disturb the body any further. He didn't want the doctor to examine Zona or do an autopsy to find out what killed her. The doctor thought he saw a strange bruise on Zona's neck, but Trout was her husband and seemed distressed, so he agreed.

Trout arranged Zona's body in her casket, again not allowing anyone to help. He pillowed her head and even wrapped her favorite scarf or veil around her neck. He stayed by her head and made a big show of crying over her if anyone came close. Zona was quickly buried in the same dress she'd been married in just a few months earlier.

That's when the haunting started. Zona's mother, Mary Jane, felt uneasy about Zona's death. She said she prayed to

know what had happened to Zona. This was a very religious
time, but not everyone viewed religion the same way. Some
believed that ghosts could communicate with the living,
while others did not. Mary Jane must have belonged to the
first group. She claimed that Zona's ghost appeared to her.
Zona announced that she had not fainted or had a heart
attack. Her husband Trout had choked her and broken her
neck.

*Wedding photo of Zona Heaster and Trout Shue. Public
domain image courtesy of West Virginia's WBOY 12 News.*

According to the *Greenbriar Independent*, Mary Jane later
testified, "It was no dream. [Zona] came back and told me
that [Trout] was mad that she didn't have no meat cooked
for supper... She said for me to look right at the right-hand
side of the door as you go in and at the right-hand corner as
you go in. Well, I saw the place just exactly as she told me,
and I saw blood right there where she told me..."

More than that, she said, "I told them [the investigators]
the very dress that she was killed in, and when she went to
leave me she turned her head completely around and looked
at me like she wanted me to know all about it."

Of course, Trout denied he had hurt Zona. But Mary Jane told the doctor about the visits from the ghost and the blood she found—just where the ghost told her to look. It was enough for authorities to dig up Zona's body for a more thorough examination. The doctor found that Zona's neck had been choked and broken, just as Mary Jane said.

The case went to trial. The prosecutors showed that no one except Trout had been at the house that morning, and that he had kept the doctor or anyone else from examining Zona carefully for the cause of her death. After the funeral, he suddenly seemed very cheerful.

Also, it turned out Trout had been married twice before. One wife was able to divorce him after he abused and then abandoned her (abandonment was a cause for divorce, even if abuse wasn't). The second had died of an "accident" when he dropped something heavy on her head. He had bragged that he was going to have seven wives in his lifetime, and Zona was number three. All these things made him look guilty, but especially the evidence of Zona's injured body. Mary Jane's testimony about Zona's ghost may have been the strongest and strangest part of the trial.

The jury quickly returned a verdict of guilty.

Trout was sentenced to prison for the rest of his life— which ended up being very short. He died a few years later of influenza.

A few of Trout's family members didn't believe he would have killed his wife, but most people felt this is a pretty clear-cut case of abuse turning to murder—and maybe even that Trout was a serial wife killer.

This is an unusual story, but where is the mystery?

It lies in Mary Jane's story of Zona's ghost. If you believe in ghosts, you might have no trouble imagining that a murdered young woman's spirit would return to her mother to reveal the truth of her death. Mary Jane asserted again and again under oath that she did see Zona—not in a dream, but in person. It certainly makes a sensational case—the only recorded account of a ghost getting justice against a murderer.

Yet those who don't believe in ghosts, or don't believe ghosts can come back to speak to the living, think there must be another explanation for how Mary Jane knew about Zona's death. Mary Jane didn't live close to Zona, so she couldn't have witnessed the murder. Some people think Mary Jane might have actually been a clever detective.

Mary Jane had never liked Trout. She objected to the wedding. Trout was cruel to her after her daughter's death, too, not allowing Mary Jane to help prepare her daughter for burial and refusing to return a ring that had belonged to her daughter.

Mary Jane, in the *Greenbriar Independent*, said of Trout, "He gave me a ring that he pretended [Zona] wanted me to have; but I don't know what dead woman he might have taken it off of. I wanted her own ring and he would not let me have it."

Clearly, there was bad blood between the mother and son-in-law. Was he taunting Mary Jane by giving her a ring that was not Zona's—that perhaps belonged to one of his previous wives?

Mary Jane was suspicious and perhaps angry. That's what she said led her to pray about Zona's death.

It's possible that in addition to praying, she did some sleuthing. Maybe she snuck over to visit Trout's house and talk to some of the locals, gathering evidence that he had been cruel to her daughter. Maybe Zona had told her mother before her death that he was abusive and that she was afraid. Maybe Mary Jane had noticed something wrong with her daughter's neck at the funeral.

When asked if she had even seen the house where her daughter lived and was killed, she said, "No, sir, I had not; but I found them just exactly as she told me it was, and I never laid eyes on that house until since her death. She told me this before I knew anything of the buildings at all."

It might be true that she never saw the house before Zona's death, but it doesn't mean she didn't explore it after. She found Zona's blood there. Did a ghost lead her to it, or was it her own investigating?

There's no evidence that Mary Jane made up the story about the ghost. Some ghost-doubters have suggested that her subconscious created Zona's ghost to help her explain what she believed had happened. In this theory, the "ghost" was her own mind putting together the evidence. It would explain how she testified so convincingly about her daughter's ghost.

But Mary Jane also might have been a clever woman working in a world that did not take women very seriously. When she reported her concerns about Zona's death to the authorities, her brother-in-law went with her. A woman's word would not be taken seriously by many men at the time. She needed a man to help back up her concerns. But even if men could ignore a mother's concerns, it was much more difficult to ignore the testimony of a ghost. Perhaps Mary Jane knew this and used it to make people listen to her suspicions about Trout.

What do you think? Can ghosts come back to bring truth and justice to the living? Or was Mary Jane using the tools available to her to solve her daughter's murder?

CHAPTER TEN

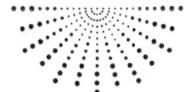

The Trial of Joe Hill

Imagine you're serving on a jury in Utah in 1914. Your job: to decide if the man sitting in front of you is guilty of murder, or if he's being framed for a crime he didn't commit. Look at the arguments and evidence and decide what you think should be the fate of Joe Hill.

On January 10, 1914, masked bandits killed grocery store owner and former policeman John G. Morrison and his seventeen-year-old son John Arling Morrison in their Salt Lake City store. Morrison's thirteen-year-old son Merlin witnessed the killing and described what happened to the *Salt Lake Tribune*:

"When the men rushed in, we all turned to see who they were. Without giving my father a moment's warning, the first one rushed to a point about opposite the scales, there, and yelled: 'We've got you now.' The shots followed. It was all so sudden that it is hard to remember. As father fell, my brother turned around to the shelf by the icebox... There was a revolver there, and he picked it up... and shot. I think the bullet hit one man. They wheeled and fired at my brother three times. He fell right there by the scales back of the counter. The men realized, I guess, what a noise they had made, for they didn't stop, but rushed right out again."

Merlin couldn't identify the men because their hats and red bandanas hid their faces. The bandits didn't steal anything, and police first suspected the killing was motivated by revenge against the former police officer. They questioned several known criminals and enemies of Morrison but couldn't prove that any of them were the killers.

The night of the shooting, a man who called himself Joe Hill staggered into a doctor's office in nearby Murray with a gunshot wound to the lung. He was wearing a pistol in a holster and claimed he'd been in a gunfight over a woman, but he wouldn't say anything else.

The doctor treated Joe Hill, but when he heard that the police were looking for someone with a wound to the chest, he told them about his late-night patient. When the police found Hill, they also found a red bandana like the one Morrison's killers had worn. His pistol had disappeared. Hill claimed he'd tossed it away.

Photo of Joe Hill courtesy of Utah State Archives and Wikimedia.

The police investigated Joe Hill. They learned his real name was Joel Häggland, though he also went by the alias Joseph Hillstrom. He was a Swedish immigrant who'd worked a variety of factory and manual labor jobs around the US. He also had a criminal record. He'd been arrested for vagrancy (being homeless) in California. He was suspected of robbing a streetcar there with his friend Otto Applequist, though he and Applequist had never been charged due to lack of evidence. Hill had gone to Mexico in 1911 with other laborers to fight in the Mexican Revolution against the corrupt government. He and other labor leaders had hoped to turn Baja California into a free state run by workers. Hill returned to the US when their plans fell through.

In fact, Joe Hill was a celebrity among workers and labor unions. He had a long history of speaking up for workers who were treated unfairly.

Hill's father died when he was only nine, and he'd been forced to quit school and work long days in a rope factory just to survive. This wasn't uncommon in the early 1900s. Workers spent long days in dangerous factories and mines for very little pay and with few safety protections—even children. In 1911, 146 men, women, and teenagers burned to death when the Triangle Shirtwaist Factory in New York caught fire. The exit doors were locked to prevent workers from taking bathroom breaks, and there were no fire extinguishers or other safety measures in the building. Some of the victims jumped from the ten-story building trying to escape. Others died desperately attempting to open the locked doors. The youngest victims were fourteen. They had worked in that factory for thirteen hours a day, seven days a week and made only $6 per week.

Workers were trapped in the top of the Triangle Shirtwaist building because their bosses had locked them in to prevent bathroom breaks. Image courtesy of Wikimedia.

Such terrible working conditions and gruesome deaths were common in the United States in the early 1900s, with hundreds of workers dying in industrial accidents every month. Almost one-fourth of children and young teenagers worked in factories, mines, and other manual labor occupations, and many would spend their whole life in such jobs—however long that life might be. There was no retirement for laborers. If they couldn't work because of old age, sickness, or injury, they and their families might starve.

These children and teenagers working in a mine in 1908 would likely spend their entire lives mining—and their lives would not be very long. Image courtesy of the Library of Congress and Wikimedia.

Joe Hill wanted to see that change. He joined labor unions and workers' organizations that encouraged workers to protest and go on strike to try to get better pay and improved working conditions. He quickly became a leader in the labor movement. That was probably why he used several different names—bosses considered him a troublemaker and wouldn't hire him under his own name.

Joe Hill liked making that kind of trouble. He was a talented musician and wrote a number of songs that were popular with working people. He invented the phrase "pie in the sky," still used today to mean a goal you can't reach. Many of the songs made fun of bosses and encouraged people to go on strike. They were often sung by striking workers.

For instance, "Workers of the World, Awaken!" says:

Workers of the world, awaken!
Break your chains, demand your rights.
All the wealth you make is taken
By exploiting parasites.
Shall you kneel in deep submission
From your cradles to your graves?
Is the height of your ambition
To be good and willing slaves?

Hill also drew cartoons. After the shooting, one was found in the room he shared with his friend Applequist, showing a masked robber gunning down a policeman.

Labor unions had a bad reputation in the United States. Some laborers marched and went on strike because their conditions were terrible. All they wanted was to be treated more fairly, with shorter working days, safer conditions, and better pay. Other labor organizers went further. Some wanted to change the entire system to socialism or communism, making it so workers owned the factories, or so that no one owned anything and everything belonged to "the people." This frightened people who owned businesses, houses, and other things that they didn't want taken away or destroyed. Anarchists went the furthest. They were willing to use violence to overthrow the government, sometimes creating bombs with dynamite to sow chaos and take down political or police leaders.

The Haymarket Riot was one of the events that made some people distrust labor organizers. In 1886, someone bombed a protest where workers were demanding shorter work days, killing several police officers and bystanders. We don't know who threw the bomb, but it was a dynamite bomb like those encouraged by anarchists. Four anarchists were blamed and hanged for encouraging violence in their followers. Image courtesy of Wikimedia.

The Industrial Workers of the World, sometimes nicknamed "Wobblies," were one of these more radical groups, and Joe Hill was an influential Wobbly member and leader. This made the police more suspicious of him.

It would be hard for a Wobbly like Joe Hill to get an unbiased trial anywhere in the United States in 1914. Utah had recently seen bloody clashes between railroad workers and police that left many there unhappy with union organizers. When Joe Hill came to trial, not a single member of the jury was a worker or sympathetic to unions. The prosecuting attorney called him a parasite, robber, and murderer who refused to do honest work.

Knowing that Joe Hill was a member of a radical labor organization, the jury heard the evidence put before it in the Morrison murder trial:

- Joe Hill had a gunshot injury to the chest like the man who had robbed the store. There was a suggestion that the exit path of the bullet going through his coat showed that his hands had been raised when he was shot, which did not match young Merlin Morrison's account of the shooting.
- He had a red bandana like the men who had robbed the store.
- His friend Otto Applequist, a suspected accomplice, had vanished the night of the murder and had not been seen or heard from since.
- The gun Joe Hill had that night had vanished, so there was no way to know if it was the same type used to kill Morrison.
- Several people said he looked similar to the man who had killed Morrison, though since the killer had worn a hat and bandana, none could be certain.
- Joe Hill refused to offer an alibi for his actions that night and would not explain how he had been shot or who shot him.
- Joe Hill had no association with Morrison and no motivation for shooting him unless the killing

was a robbery gone wrong or a random attack against a former police officer.

There were a couple of pieces of evidence that the jury did not get to hear. Judges decide what information lawyers may present in a trial, and both of these were excluded.

The first was that Joe Hill had told the doctor that he'd been shot in a fight over a woman. If Joe Hill wasn't willing to testify of that himself in court, then the jury wouldn't know about it. Hill refused to offer an alibi and would not say anything about that night, whether the story about the woman was true or not.

The other was mentioned in newspaper reports of the incident but didn't come out in the trial. Morrison had told some neighbors that he was afraid someone he once arrested was coming to get revenge on him. That would not fit the description of Joe Hill, who had never met Morrison.

There's another piece of evidence that was only revealed later. Hilda Erickson, whose family owned the boarding house where both Joe Hill and Otto Applequist were staying, had been engaged to Otto Applequist at the time. She later claimed that both Hill and Applequist liked her. She said Hill told her that Applequist had shot him in an argument over her. If this is true, she never said anything while Hill's life hung in the balance—and she even attended the trial. Also, she was not a witness to the shooting. Hill could have told her Applequist shot him to hide the robbery. It does, however, fit the story Hill told the doctor on the night he was shot. If he and Applequist fought over Hilda, Hill may have been protecting her from embarrassment or a bad reputation. The question is if keeping silent about her was worth dying over.

On the other hand, the doctor who treated Hill later claimed that Hill had confessed the murder to him, saying he'd shot the Morrisons, presumably during a failed robbery, because they had guns. If this is true, however, it's strange that the doctor didn't testify at the trial.

The Utah jury found Hill guilty and condemned him to death. He chose death by firing squad.

He said, "I have been shot a few times in the past and I guess I can stand it again."

Many people did not think there was enough evidence to prove Hill was guilty. They tried to have his death sentence overturned or at least paused. Even the Swedish ambassador and the United States president, Woodrow Wilson, asked Utah's Governor Spry to delay the execution. But Spry was especially strict against labor organizers, and he insisted the sentence be carried out.

Joe Hill was shot to death in November 1915.

He sent a last message to a friend, saying, "Goodbye, Bill, I die like a true blue rebel. Don't waste any time mourning. Organize." This became a slogan for union organizers.

Hill also added, "Could you arrange to have my body hauled to the state line to be buried? I don't want to be found dead in Utah."

To this day, people debate whether Hill was guilty. Many consider him a martyr for the labor cause, victim of a system biased against labor organizers. The Fair Labor Standards Act of 1938 was a win for him and others who had fought for better working conditions. It prohibited child labor for those under 16 in most jobs, established a minimum wage, and limited normal work weeks to forty hours.

The IWW and other labor organizations continued to press for better conditions for workers. Image courtesy of the Library of Congress and Wikimedia.

No one else ever came forward with a claim to have shot Morrison, and we don't know what happened to Otto Applequist or what he thought of Joe Hill's trial and death.

Most people who think Hill is innocent suspect Frank Z. Wilson, a convicted robber arrested by Morrison who had been released shortly before the murder. Wilson's real name was Magnus Olson. Like Hill, he was a Scandinavian immigrant, so they might have had similar coloring and build. In fact, when police first arrested Hill, they thought he was Frank Wilson using a false name. Wilson later joined the gang of the notorious Al Capone in Chicago and ended up in prison. He wrote a tell-all bragging about his life of crime, but he never mentioned the Morrison case (maybe because he hadn't been caught for that crime, maybe because he wasn't involved), leaving it a mystery that may never have an answer.

So, what do you think? If you were on that jury—if you had the extra information that the jury did not—would you find Joe Hill guilty or not guilty?

CHAPTER ELEVEN

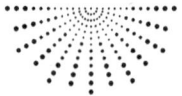

The Gangster's Secret

Dutch Schultz was not a popular man, even for a gangster. He could be charming and funny, but he had a short and violent temper, quick to get revenge on his enemies—and almost everyone was his enemy. He was so sure that everyone was out to get him that he hid his money to keep it safe. Unfortunately for him, he was right about all those enemies, and he couldn't keep himself safe. When he died, his wealth went up for grabs—if anyone could find it.

Dutch Schultz was born in the Bronx, New York City, with the less catchy name of Arthur Flegenheimer. His father abandoned the family when Schultz was in his teens, forcing him to look for ways to earn money. He decided that stealing paid better than working, which quickly landed him in prison.

One of Dutch Schultz's early mugshots. Image courtesy of Wikimedia.

When he got out, he made his way back to the streets and started up his own gang as Dutch Schultz. The nickname Dutch referred to his German (called "Deutsch") heritage, and Schultz was a reference to an earlier violent criminal.

Schultz returned to New York City at the beginning of the 1920s. In January of 1920, the US government had outlawed the sale of alcohol throughout the country. They hoped that this would stop the crime, disease, and irresponsible behavior that can come from drinking too much alcohol. Having just fought against Germany in World War I, some people also wanted to punish German beer brewers and other foreigners they believed thrived on liquor.

Just because alcohol was illegal didn't mean no one wanted to drink it, though. Even some of the politicians who voted for Prohibition still drank (they didn't want other people to have alcohol, but they were fine with it for themselves and their friends). Some people tried making their own alcohol. This often ended badly, with people blinded or killed by poisonous liquor. Others looked for people willing to sell them alcohol illegally.

That was where Dutch Schultz and other gangsters stepped in. Gangsters smuggled liquor in from places where it was legal, like Canada. They sold it in secret clubs called speakeasies. People looking for alcohol would ask around until a friend told them the location of one of these secret hangouts. They were often in the basements of legal businesses or even houses, maybe protected by hidden tunnels and false walls.

Once the guest gave the right password at the door, he or she entered the club. The air was full of cigarette smoke and the sour scent of alcohol. The fast pulse of jazz music pumped through the room. For people still traumatized by World War I and the Spanish Flu, visiting speakeasies might offer a distraction from bad memories or worries about the future. The gangsters quickly became rich and powerful, making millions of dollars a year at a time when most of the country was sliding into the hunger and poverty of the Great Depression.

These young people are waiting to slip into a speakeasy in Washington, D.C. Image courtesy of the Library of Congress.

Of course, the police and the new Federal Bureau of Investigation (FBI) tried to stop the gangsters. This sometimes led to violent confrontations and gunfights. Because so much money was at stake, gangs also fought each other over the areas or territories where they ran their speakeasies. They even forced businesses in their territories to pay them "protection money" or else risk being beaten or seeing their businesses smashed or burned.

Crime and violence increased as the gangs became more powerful. Dutch Schultz and his blazing temper quickly flared to the top, brutal even by mobster standards. He murdered members of rival gangs to take their territories, and he tortured people who would not buy alcohol from him, beating and blinding them.

By the 1930s, people had had enough. The government repealed Prohibition in 1933, admitting that it caused far more problems than it solved. Local police were sometimes scared of, overwhelmed by, or even controlled by mob bosses, so the Federal Bureau of Investigation (FBI) stepped in. Federal officials had trouble sending the gangsters to prison for their worst illegal activities, though. Gangsters protected each other from federal agents, refusing to testify even against their rivals.

The government found another way to get mob bosses into prison: tax fraud. Mob bosses accumulated their vast illegal fortunes while running legal businesses like restaurants that were fronts for their criminal activities. They might pay taxes on the smaller amounts that they earned from their fronts, but not on the money that they stole, extorted, and otherwise earned illegally. It was easy to show that the mob bosses had much more money than they brought in legally and paid taxes on. In 1931, famous Chicago gangster Al Capone, also known as Scarface, went to prison for tax fraud.

Tax fraud finally took down notorious crime boss Al Capone. Mugshot courtesy of Wikimedia.

The FBI then set its sights on Dutch Schultz.

Schultz was already unpopular even among other gangsters for his temper. He threatened to murder Thomas Dewey, the lawyer who was working to prosecute him for tax fraud. Such a murder would draw even more federal attention to gangsters, and the rest of the New York City mob bosses didn't want that, so they refused to support Schultz. Dewey had already put several New York gangsters in prison, and the clock was ticking for Schultz.

The brutal mob boss sensed that the sharks were circling and that no one had his back. He had never trusted banks—he'd probably robbed his share of them—so he kept all of his money in safes. He couldn't keep money at his house anymore, though, since Dewey or the FBI would seize it.

Schultz had a hideout in the Catskill Mountains of New York where he hid smuggled alcohol and lay low when the police were getting too close. His hideout had secret tunnels and hidden rooms to make and store liquor. The Catskills are north of New York City, and a very different world from the "concrete jungle" of the city. The area is 700,000 acres of forests, rivers, and mountain peaks, very isolated. It was into this wilderness that people believe Schultz and his trusted bodyguard, "Lulu," took millions of dollars' worth of money and gold to keep it safe. Schultz supposedly dropped a hint that the fortune wasn't on his property, but on someone else's, who wouldn't even know the treasure was there.

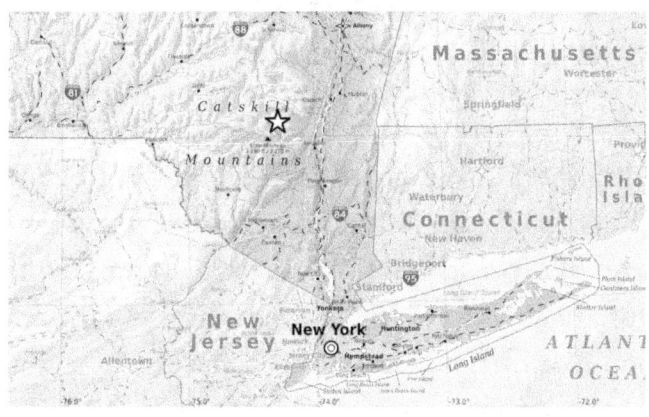

The star on this map shows the approximate location of Dutch Schultz's hideout in the Catskills. Image based on a map by OpenStreetMap and Wikimedia, CC BY SA 4.0.

Schultz may have hidden his wealth, but he didn't hide his ongoing plans to kill Dewey. The other local mob bosses were tired of Schultz's threats and violence and the danger he brought to all of their businesses. They decided on the extreme solution of sending hitmen to stop him. The hitmen cornered Schultz in the men's bathroom of one of his restaurants and shot him and his bodyguards, including Lulu.

Dutch Schultz's threats against Thomas Dewey made him dangerous to other mobsters. Image courtesy of Wikimedia.

Schultz and Lulu lingered for several days before dying. Schultz babbled while fading in and out of awareness. The Internet Archive preserved the transcript of his last words.

Below are just some of his ramblings—ramblings that some people think hold clues to the treasure.

"Whose number is that in your pocketbook, Phil 13780?"

"Two thousand. Come on, get some money in that treasury. We need it."

"Mother is the best bet, and don't let Satan draw you too fast."

"Him? John? Over a million, five million dollars."

"If you do this, you can go on and jump right here in the lake. I know who they are. They are French people."

"Who gets it? I don't know and I don't want to know, but look out. It can be traced."

It's not in the transcripts, but it's widely reported that at some point, Schultz said, "Don't be a dope Lulu, we better get those Liberty bonds out of the box and cash 'em," and "Wonder who owns these woods? He'll never know what's buried in 'em."

And from his last recorded response when police asked him who shot him:

"I know what I am doing here with my collection of papers. It isn't worth a nickel to two guys like you or me, but to a collector, it is worth a fortune. It is priceless. I am going to turn it over to... Look out. I want that G-note [a thousand dollars]. Come on, open the soap duckets. The chimney sweeps. Talk to the sword... French-Canadian bean soup. I want to pay. Let them leave me alone."

Those were Dutch Schultz's last words. He slipped into a coma and died a couple of hours later. He was thirty-four years old. Reportedly, his vast fortune was missing, and rumors immediately began to swirl. Some people said Lulu had made a map of where they buried the fortune for Schultz's next in command, Marty Krompier. But Krompier was shot soon after Schultz, and if the map did exist, it's now missing.

Locals reported seeing Schultz and Lulu in the Catskills near the town of Phoenicia shortly before he was shot, heading up Highway 214.

This is in the same area where Schultz had his hideout.

Some try to connect any clues in his final ramblings with the location of the treasure. Is it related to the code 13780? Is the treasure actually in French Canada and not New York? Schultz and Lulu were seen lying low in Bridgeport, Connecticut about a month before their deaths, so they weren't only hiding in New York. Does his reference to "don't let Satan draw you too fast" mean the treasure is close to Phoenicia-area landmarks the Devil's Face or Devil's Tombstone? What about in a lake?

Do soap, chimneys, swords, or bean soup offer any clues, or were they just delirious ramblings of a brain that was shutting down? If someone finds the treasure, it may all make sense, but until that day, we can only wonder.

Schultz also mentioned his mother and his sister Helen. If they knew anything about the fortune, they kept it very quiet.

Ever since Schultz's death, treasure hunters have been searching the Catskills for his lost treasure. If anyone has found anything, they haven't told. Phoenician residents are tired of people digging up their yards, but most searchers reason that Schultz was a city boy and wouldn't have traveled far from the pockets of civilization along the road. If Schultz went farther afield, there are still thousands of acres to search. If he hid the metal box in water, it could be buried under almost a century of mud or washed downstream. Still, the treasure may be waiting for some lucky person to find the right clues and uncover its location.

The Catskills are a huge area to search for treasure. Image courtesy of Daniel Case and Wikimedia, GNU license.

CHAPTER TWELVE

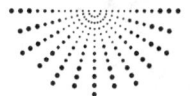

The Ghost Blimp of World War II

August 16, 1942. It was supposed to be a routine mission. With morning dew still clinging to the ground, the US Navy's L-8 blimp prepared to depart San Francisco for a four-hour flight as part of homeland defense in World War II.

The blimp would drift back to San Francisco about five hours later—without its two pilots. The two men vanished from the blimp without a trace, while ships and airplanes watched, creating one of the enduring mysteries of World War II.

The L-8's assignment was to search for Japanese submarines along the California coast. Since Japan had bombed Pearl Harbor in Hawaii on December 7, 1941, drawing the US into World War II, several Japanese subs had been spotted off the West Coast of the United States. One had shelled an oil field near Santa Barbara, California in February 1942. In June, another had fired on Fort Stevens on the Oregon Coast, and Japanese forces then stormed the Aleutian Islands in Alaska.

Pearl Harbor brought the United States into World War II. Image courtesy of NARA and Wikimedia.

These events, combined with Japanese submarine attacks on US ships in the Pacific, sent the West Coast into high alert. The day after the shelling in Santa Barbara, an escaped US weather balloon set off a mass panic in the middle of the night known as The Battle of Los Angeles. Military personnel fired anti-aircraft guns at the weather balloon, and everyone thought the city was under attack, sometimes shooting at each other in the darkness. Only in the morning did it become clear that there were no Japanese planes over the city.

The "Battle of Los Angeles" was the result of panic and miscommunication. Image courtesy of the Associated Press and Wikimedia.

Also in 1942, about 120,000 Japanese immigrants and Japanese-American citizens living along the West Coast were forced to abandon their homes and businesses and imprisoned in internment camps in the deserts of California, Utah, and Idaho in fear that they might help Japanese invaders.

What would you pack if you were forced to leave your home for a prison camp? Image by Ansel Adams, courtesy of the Library of Congress.

It was in this atmosphere of fear that the L-8 readied for its mission. Its two pilots were experienced airshipmen. The pilot was Lieutenant Ernest "Ernie" D. Cody, a 27-year-old graduate of the US Naval Academy. He had already made a name for himself as an airship pilot by performing a tricky supply drop from a blimp to an aircraft carrier on the open sea. The co-pilot was 34-year-old Ensign Charles Ellis Adams who had over ten years and 2,000 hours of experience working with blimps. In fact, he had already survived one airship crash when the *USS Macon* went down off the California coast in 1935. He had also been one of the rescuers after the *Hindenburg* disaster, when a zeppelin-style airship had exploded while attempting to land at Lakehurst Naval Air Station.

The terrible explosion of the Hindenburg *turned people away from airship travel. Image courtesy of the US Navy and Wikimedia.*

Unlike the *Hindenburg*, which had a rigid body filled with explosive hydrogen gas, the L-8 had a soft body filled with helium. Helium is still light enough to float but not explosive. It's not as light as hydrogen, however, and can't carry as much weight.

On that August morning, there was enough dew on the airship that it was slow taking off. Twenty-year-old mechanic James Riley Hill boarded the gondola that carried the crew beneath the airship for the morning flight.

The gondola of the L-8 in the Naval Aviation Museum.
Photo courtesy of the Naval Aviation Museum.

Hill told the Imperial Valley Press a couple of days later, "I was posted for this flight and was on hand for the takeoff. I took my seat and closed the door. We were already moving when Mr. Cody decided that because of a static condition the ship couldn't carry the weight of three men and ordered me out. I jumped from the ship."

The blimp floated away at about 6 a.m. Hill probably considered himself very lucky before the day was over.

The airship headed toward the Farallon Islands off the coast of San Francisco. These small islands are now a protected marine sanctuary for seals, sea birds, and other marine life, but during World War II, they were home to a Navy radio station attempting to track the signals of Japanese ships.

The airship checked in with its base at 7:38 a.m. to announce it was near the Farallon Islands.

Then at about 7:42, Cody sent his last known message: "Investigating suspicious oil slick—stand by."

Oil slicks often indicated the presence of Japanese submarines.

Several ships had been in the area where the blimp investigated the oil slick. The blimp was a familiar sight, and the local Navy and Coast Guard patrol ships and fishing vessels knew it was watching for submarines, so they paid attention to its actions. After the time that the L-8 sent its last message about the oil slick sighting, nearby ships witnessed someone drop two smoke flares to mark the position of the oil.

Fifteen minutes after that initial report, the commanders at the base in San Francisco wanted an update from the L-8. They tried to contact it, but no one responded.

The blimp then circled for about an hour. It mostly stayed at 200 to 300 feet above the water, but at one point it circled much lower—to no more than 30 feet, and perhaps just skimming over the choppy, grey ocean waves. The watching ships wondered what the blimp was doing. The finishing boats pulled back. The military vessels readied their guns in case the L-8 had spotted a submarine and was preparing to drop one of its depth charges.

Yet instead of deploying a charge, the airship dropped ballast—the weight that helped keep it low—and headed up into the clouds as if returning to San Francisco.

By this time, the base was very concerned that they hadn't heard from the blimp. They asked any planes in the area to report on the blimp and also sent out their own planes to search for it.

A civilian seaplane reported seeing the L-8 returning to San Francisco. Then one of the Navy search planes spotted it high above the clouds at 2000 feet. Helium expands as it goes higher in the atmosphere, so if the blimp went any higher, it would have to vent helium to avoid popping.

The blimp was next spotted approaching the shore.

By the time the L-8 returned to shore, it had lost helium and was sagging. Photo courtesy of the National Archives.

The *Imperial Valley Press* reported that Ida Ruby had witnessed the blimp's return.

She said, "I noticed the blimp out over the water. It was very low... the entire blimp seemed to be folding into a rough V-shape. It was drifting in toward the beach with the wind. I watched it with binoculars and was quite sure I could see three persons in the cabin."

The *Imperial Valley Press* also wrote, "Edward Taylor, 17, said he watched the blimp through binoculars and said he thought he saw men moving about inside it."

At 10:45, someone called in a report that the airship had been spotted at the beach. Two men outside the blimp wrestled with its ropes, trying to control it. The blimp, drifting low after having vented helium, rammed into a cliffside, clogging the engine with dirt and knocking loose one of its depth charges—an explosive used to attack submarines. The depth charge didn't explode (they are activated by water pressure), but losing that extra weight allowed the blimp to rise and sail on.

The blimp continued on and crash-landed in nearby Daly City, California.

The *Imperial Valley Press,* on the day after the incident, included a witness statement that, "I could hear the wheels roll across the roof. Then it struck the electric wires and there was a big flash. It settled down in the street."

In fact, it landed on top of someone's empty car. Thankfully, no one was hurt. But the blimp's gondola was empty.

The empty blimp crashed in Daly City. Image courtesy of the National Archives.

The Navy initially thought the two men spotted on the beach with the blimp had been the pilots, but it turned out they were two fishermen or swimmers who had tried to capture the blimp when it drifted back to land.

When the blimp landed in Daly City, the only things missing from inside the gondola were two of its lifejackets, which the pilots were required to wear, and the two smoke flares the blimp had dropped at the oil slick. The classified documents were in place. The investigators found dust in the bottom of the gondola that indicated it had never gotten wet. Cody's hat was sitting on the controls. The radio was functional, with the speaker hanging out of the door, but its battery was dead. One of the engines was turned on full, and the other was halfway on. The door was open and secured in such a way that it seemed it must have been latched from the outside.

The Navy sent out a search party for the two men, assuming they must be in the water. Even if they had died, their bodies should have floated in their life jackets.

The search found nothing.

The Navy then hoped that the men had been picked up by another ship that was maintaining radio silence to avoid detection by enemy submarines. It was soon clear, however, that no US ships had found the Navy pilots. The two men had vanished.

The men who saw the blimp circle the oil slick were confident that the pilots were steering the blimp while they watched. Likewise, the planes that spotted the blimp flying extra high thought it seemed to be under pilot control. When it neared the beach, observers thought they saw the pilots on board. But by the time it landed, the pilots were both missing along with their life jackets.

So, what happened to the missing men? No trace of them was ever found, and we're left with only guesses.

Some people suggested a rogue wave caught the airship and knocked the men out, but it was dry and dusty inside.

The Navy found that the door latch might have been faulty, so if co-pilot Adams had leaned on the door, he might have tumbled out. Adams also could have lost his balance when he dropped the smoke flares. Or perhaps he fell while checking on the engines, since they'd left their mechanic behind. After all, one of the engines was set to full and the other to only half, which could indicate a mechanical problem. Any of these things might have caused Adams to fall from the blimp.

Regardless of the cause, if Adams fell, Cody might have reacted out of instinct and tried to grab him, then they both fell into the water. Perhaps the blimp circling low over the water was Cody's attempt to rescue Adams. Maybe what onlookers thought was ballast dropping from the ship was actually a person. Losing the weight of two people from the ship would have caused it to suddenly float higher, which fits eyewitness accounts of the ship's actions.

Skeptics of this theory point out that many people on several ships were watching the blimp closely at the time it was circling the water. How could they have failed to notice two men falling from the airship? Would they really have mistaken a tumbling human body for ballast? And would Cody have bothered to leave his hat behind on the controls if he jumped to Adams' rescue?

Furthermore, the theory that the men fell out of the ship doesn't explain why the pilots weren't responding to the radio while they were still circling the oil slick. If Adams had fallen through the door—even if he was hanging on—Cody's training would have been to radio the situation in so someone could come rescue Adams. One of the Navy's rules, then as well as now, was for men to never abandon their ships. Maybe the radio died and Cody tried to save Adams.

But then why was the radio speaker dangling outside the ship?

One explanation for Cody's behavior speculates that the men were testing a new kind of radar system using microwave radiation. The radiation might have made the men ill and confused so they fell from the ship. But there's no evidence that the L-8 was using such technology, and there's still the problem of no one seeing the men fall.

They could have fallen from the ship on their way back to base, which might have made them harder to spot. Some have speculated that they got into a fight about something. If they did fight, they both might have fallen from the ship. Or, one man killed the other, rolled him out of the gondola, and then escaped to start a new life somewhere else. It's not impossible, but there's no proof of it.

Any suggestions about the men falling from the blimp has to explain what happened to the pilots and their life jackets. An extensive search of the area turned up no signs of the men or their bodies. Even if they were knocked unconscious or killed by the fall, the life jackets should have made them easy to find, especially if they fell out near the oil slick. If they fell out once the blimp returned to land, why did they allow it to drift so high and cut off radio communication?

The fact that the door was latched open and that Ida Ruby said she saw three people in the blimp has led to theories about sabotage and spies. Some suggest that maybe a spy or stowaway got into the gondola, took over the L-8, and killed the pilots at some point. But the airship gondola is pretty small for anyone to hide in.

The witness testimonies are tricky. The blimp was folding in on itself into a V and drifting low because it had lost helium by flying too high—something that would have been strange for the pilots to allow. Yet Taylor thought people were moving in the airship, and Ruby believed there were not two but three people in the gondola. Maybe that is what they saw and it's part of the mystery. But our eyes and our memory can play tricks on us, sometimes making us see what we expect to see. People were frightened and on the lookout for strange or threatening occurrences—both Ida Ruby and Edward Taylor were carrying binoculars around with them.

Also, the airship was very sensitive to weight—a third man was already left behind because the ship was too heavy and had trouble taking off.

Or was there another reason?

What if Cody didn't want the mechanic on the ship because he or both pilots were doing something illegal? Some think one or both men were spying for the Japanese. Maybe when the ship circled low, they were exchanging information. Sending a message to a Japanese submarine could explain why the radio speaker was dangling from the gondola, and even why the men didn't respond to the radio messages from base. Then, the theory goes, the blimp moved out of sight, and either both men defected, or one man killed the other and ran off. Yet the nearby ships saw no submarine, the Navy radio station heard no Japanese transmissions, and no evidence has come to light in the decades since the war that the men worked for the Japanese. Also, if one or both men were spies, why would they leave behind the classified documents? And why defect at a point when they were in positions of trust and no one suspected them? Adams had just been commissioned an ensign the weekend before the flight.

The door latched open from the outside is one of several strange facts about this mystery, but it's also not as straightforward as it seems. It could have been latched open by one of the rescuers after the ship had landed. The rescuers also sliced open the blimp's helium envelope to make certain no one was trapped beneath it. Not knowing the blimp was empty, they acted quickly to try to rescue any survivors, but they might have accidentally erased or altered some clues.

None of the theories perfectly explains what happened to the pilots of the L-8, especially since no trace of them was ever found. The US Navy decided that the men must have fallen out of the blimp...somehow. The government declared them dead. But we may never know what actually happened on the L-8 that fateful day. What do you think happened to the vanished pilots?

The L-8 airship. After the war, Goodyear used the gondola as one of its "Goodyear Blimps" for advertising until it retired to the National Naval Aviation Museum. Image courtesy of the National Archives.

CHAPTER THIRTEEN

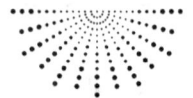

The Death of a President

There are some memories that unite a nation. Each generation has a question that brings the memories and emotions rushing back. Do you remember the COVID lockdowns in 2020? Where were you when the planes crashed into the Twin Towers on September 11, 2001? Did you watch the Challenger shuttle explode in 1986? Do you remember the first time a man walked on the moon in 1969? Did you hear the announcement when Pearl Harbor was bombed in 1941?

For almost anyone alive in the 1960s, one question looms in their memory: What moment did you hear about the assassination of President John F. Kennedy? And they probably wonder further: What was behind the murder of the president?

Kennedy was the youngest person ever elected US president at age 43. Kennedy had been a war hero in World War II. A Japanese ship rammed the small boat he commanded, sinking it. He and the other survivors helped the injured onto floating wreckage and swam everyone to the nearest island. Kennedy dragged one man by clutching his lifebelt strap in his teeth as he swam.

Kennedy and his wife Jackie portrayed youth and idealism.
Image courtesy of Everett Collection Historical via Alamy.

When Kennedy ran for president in 1960, television was just becoming a major force in American life and politics. Kennedy was considered handsome and spoke very well in front of audiences. Many saw him as a fresh start, bringing renewed idealism to America. He said, "Never before has man had such capacity to control his own environment, to end thirst and hunger, to conquer poverty and disease, to banish illiteracy and massive human misery. We have the power to make this the best generation of mankind in the history of the world - or make it the last." People later called his presidency Camelot after the legendary idealistic court of King Arthur.

As president, he set a goal to put a man on the moon and bring him safely back to earth by 1970. He also wanted to see changes in the discrimination against Black Americans, who still struggled to exercise their right to vote and were banned from some "all-White" establishments, especially in the South. He gave some support to human rights activists such as Martin Luther King, Jr.

Martin Luther King Jr.'s "I Have a Dream Speech" in August 1963 helped mobilize people for equality. Image courtesy of the Martin Luther King Jr. National Historic Sire.

He also steered the country through a tense part of the Cold War with Soviet Russia. Russia backed communism while the United States backed capitalism. Because Russia and the United States both had nuclear weapons that could devastate entire continents, though, most people feared a direct war between the two superpowers. Kennedy committed more troops to fighting against communism in Vietnam, leading to the Vietnam War. And he guided the US through the Cuban Missile Crisis. When the US discovered that Russia was building nuclear missile sites in Cuba, just off America's southern coast, it looked like the world might be on the brink of a world-ending nuclear disaster. But Kennedy was able to negotiate an end to the crisis.

Not everyone liked Kennedy. In his first speech as president, he said, "Ask not what your country can do for you...ask what you can do for your country." He was asking people to do hard things to make America better. Some didn't want to see the racial situation change in the South. Others thought he was either too easy on communism and Soviet Russia or too hard on it. He was the first Catholic US president, and some in the Protestant Christian majority felt that Catholic Christians were too foreign. He was also hiding major health problems from the public.

Even some of Kennedy's own government didn't like his policies. J. Edgar Hoover, who had been the director of the FBI since 1924, before it was even called the FBI, was one of those who wanted a stronger stand against Russia and its communist supporters in the United States. Kennedy wanted Hoover to investigate the mob and organized crime, but Hoover was focused on communists. He was against the Civil Rights leaders in the South because he suspected them of communist leanings. Hoover spied on President Kennedy, his brother Robert Kennedy, and Martin Luther King, Jr. Some people think Hoover was able to keep his job because he found out embarrassing things about the president and other powerful political leaders and blackmailed them.

From left to right, Robert Kennedy, J. Edgar Hoover, and President Kennedy. Image courtesy of Wikimedia.

Kennedy also didn't get along well with his vice president, Lyndon B. Johnson. He chose Johnson to be his vice president because Johnson had appeal in Texas and the South, where Kennedy was not popular due to his New England upbringing and views on Civil Rights. But Kennedy didn't think Johnson should ever be president, and some people believed he would drop Johnson as vice president in the 1964 elections.

On November 22, 1963, Kennedy and his wife Jackie were touring through Dallas with the Governor of Texas, John Connally, and his wife Nellie. They rode in an open-top convertible. People lined the streets, some to jeer at the president, but most to cheer for him.

Shortly before the shooting, the Kennedys in the back of the limo and the Connallys in the front. Image courtesy of Wikimedia.

As they drove through Dealey Plaza, Nellie Connally turned to Kennedy and said that no one could say that Texas didn't love him.

"No, they sure can't," Kennedy replied.

A bang rang over the plaza. Some people thought it was a firecracker. But the president grabbed his throat. A bullet had gone through his back and neck. The same bullet or a second one also hit the Governor, seated in front of Kennedy. Kennedy didn't duck or try to move, possibly because of shock, possibly he wore a stiff back brace due to an old football injury and other health problems.

Jackie checks on her husband after the first bullet struck.
Photo taken by Mary Moorman, courtesy of Wikimedia.

Then, another bang, maybe two. Everything was in confusion. Another bullet hit the president in the head. His head snapped back. Some people think this proves he was hit from the front, unlike the first shot. Others say it was an automatic reaction to the severe brain injury on the back of his head.

Mrs. Kennedy scrambled onto the trunk of the car for something. She couldn't remember later what she was doing, but she may have been grabbing a piece of his skull.

The Connallys heard her say over and over, "They have killed my husband."

One of the Secret Service agents assigned to protect the First Lady jumped onto the back of the car, attempting to shield the Kennedys. He was the only Secret Service agent to do so.

Their driver sped for Parkland Memorial Hospital, where the president was pronounced dead.

At the plaza, chaos reigned. Many people had taken cover, not knowing where the gunshots came from. Some said they thought the shots came from the book depository building overlooking the street. Others believed the shots came from the grassy knoll in the plaza. A search of the grassy knoll uncovered no sign of a gunman, but several witnesses saw a shooter in the sixth-floor window of the depository building.

Police officers found a rifle by the sixth-floor depository window. It matched all the bullets recovered at the scene. Lee Harvey Oswald was immediately a suspect because he worked at the depository and went missing right after the shooting. He'd been in the US Marines but was court-martialed for fighting and later discharged. He'd then tried to defect to the Soviet Union and married there before returning with his Russian wife to Dallas. Back in the US, he tried to assassinate an anti-communist speaker and promoted communist Cuba, though officials supposedly didn't know these things until after Kennedy's assassination. He'd also traveled to Mexico City shortly before the shooting and may have visited the Russian and Cuban embassies there. Oswald was soon arrested at a theater, where he tried to watch a movie while the rest of the city was in a furor over the assassination.

Meanwhile, Vice President Lyndon Johnson was told that he was now the president. He needed to be sworn in and return to Washington, D.C. Johnson wouldn't act until he had confirmation that the president was dead, and then he didn't want to leave Mrs. Kennedy in Texas.

This led to a riotous scene at the hospital. The coroner there wanted to perform the autopsy immediately. Kennedy's aides wanted to take the body back to Washington, D.C. The aides attacked the coroner. He didn't want to make more of a scene, so he allowed them to put the body in a coffin and take it away without being examined.

With the coffin on Air Force One, both Mrs. Kennedy and Lyndon Johnson boarded, and Johnson was sworn in as president.

Lyndon B. Johnson is sworn in as president on Air Force One. Jackie Kennedy stands beside him, still wearing the dress stained with her husband's blood. Image courtesy of Wikimedia.

In Washington, D.C., Mrs. Kennedy chose Bethesda Naval Hospital to perform the autopsy. Under pressure to work quickly, the doctors there performed a hasty autopsy certifying that the president had been killed by a bullet to the head. The original autopsy report was destroyed, supposedly because it had the president's blood stains on it. They saved the president's brain for further study, but it went missing. Some people think a member of the Kennedy family took or destroyed it and other autopsy evidence so people wouldn't find out about the numerous health problems Kennedy had hidden from the public. Others say the original report and the brain would have proved that the assassination wasn't all it seemed to be.

Two days after the autopsy, while the nation prepared for the funeral, a Dallas nightclub owner named Jack Ruby shot and killed Lee Harvey Oswald as he was being transferred to a different jail. Ruby claimed he did it so Mrs. Kennedy wouldn't have to suffer through a trial. Yet Ruby was known to have associations with organized crime.

Conspiracy theories began to swirl. Did Lee Harvey Oswald really work alone? Did Jack Ruby? The government instituted the Warren Commission to examine these questions. It concluded that Lee Harvey Oswald was the only shooter and acted alone. But many people question the Warren Commission's findings, leaving a number of questions unanswered.

Why did someone call the embassy in Mexico using Lee Harvey Oswald's name shortly before the assassination? Later examination suggested it wasn't Oswald who made the call, so why did someone pretend to be him?

Did a spy in London know about the assassination ahead of time? Supposedly, a British spy warned that he had big news about Kennedy the morning before the shooting, but no one acted on it.

In fact, a week before the assassination in Dallas, citizens in Chicago foiled another assassination attempt there by reporting suspicious behavior of a man who planned to kill Kennedy.

But if Kennedy was in so much danger, why was he not protected better?

Who were the witnesses who never came forward? Though the government gathered many photographs and films from witnesses at the plaza, some remain missing. The most notable was a woman wearing a trench coat despite the heat, whose face was hidden by a headscarf and sunglasses. She is seen in other photographs apparently filming or taking pictures calmly during the shooting while other people scramble for cover. She is called "Babushka Lady" for her scarf's resemblance to a Russian head covering worn by "babushkas" or older women. We don't know for certain, however, that the figure was a woman instead of a man in disguise.

Despite a long search, Babushka Lady and whatever images she (or he) has of the assassination are still a mystery.

A still from the Marie Muchmore film just before the assassination shows the "Babushka Lady" filming or taking pictures. Image courtesy of the Internet Archive.

This still from the Mark Bell film just after the assassination shows all the bystanders on the ground except the "Babushka Lady," who may still be holding up her camera.

Were Kennedy and Connally really hit by the same bullet? The first shot supposedly hit both Kennedy and Connally, but the path of the bullet seems to bounce around a lot. Depending on the angle that Connally was sitting, it's possible that a bullet could have hit both of them, but some people doubt this. That bullet stayed lodged in the governor and was buried with him when he died. Many wanted to remove the bullet and test it after he died, but his family refused. If the bullet was retrieved, would it match the other bullets and Oswald's gun?

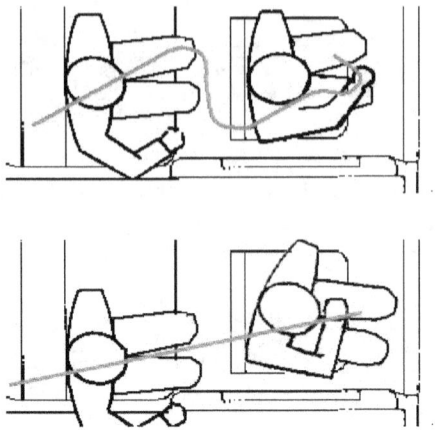

The angle that Kennedy and Connally sat in would determine if the same bullet could have hit them both. Image courtesy of bradipus and Wikimedia.

Let's look at the most common theories for those who don't believe that Lee Harvey Oswald acted alone.

Many at the time thought communists might be involved in killing Kennedy. Oswald was part of the movement that wanted communist Cuba to be free from American interference. In Mexico City, he met Russians and possibly Cubans. He might have believed that he could flee to Cuba or Russia and be welcomed as a hero for assassinating the American president. In fact, in his earlier attempt to assassinate the anti-communist general, he left a note for his wife telling her that Russia would take care of her if he were caught.

Opponents of this theory point out that Russia was very

quick to assure the United States that it had nothing to do with the assassination. Of course, they probably would have said this even if they had assassinated him. But Russia did not want a war with the United States because it almost certainly would have been a nuclear war with devastating consequences for both sides.

Some people blame organized crime for Kennedy's death. After all, he was pushing J. Edgar Hoover to investigate the mob more carefully. And Jack Ruby had associations with organized crime. Rumors also said that mobster Sam Giancana had helped Kennedy win the election. CIA files show that the government tried to work with Giancana and the mob to assassinate Fidel Castro, the dictator of Cuba. Those who believe this theory think that maybe the mob was upset that Kennedy decided to crack down on them.

What about white supremacists like the Ku Klux Klan who wanted to keep Black people and other non-White and non-Protestant groups from gaining more power? They already didn't like Catholics like Kennedy, and he was helping the Civil Rights movement.

When Ruby Bridges was one of a few Black children selected to help integrate all-White schools in Louisiana in 1960, it required several U.S. Marshals to keep her safe because of racial prejudice. Image courtesy of the Department of Justice and Wikimedia.

Could J. Edgar Hoover, Lyndon Johnson, or both have been involved in a plot to kill Kennedy? Johnson didn't want to lose his position as vice president, and Hoover didn't like Kennedy. Even more, Hoover was about to turn 70, and the law at the time required federal employees to retire at that age. Hoover didn't want to retire and let go of his power.

Johnson and Hoover both gained something from Kennedy's death, but that doesn't mean they were behind it. It is interesting to note, however, that J. Edgar Hoover knew about threats to Martin Luther King, Jr. that he refused to pass on. Could he have done the same with Kennedy? It's strange that Oswald was able to pull of an assassination when he was already under government surveillance after his return from Russia and his trip to Mexico City. After the assassination, Hoover emphasized the importance of people believing Oswald acted alone. Was that because it was true, or was it just what Hoover wanted people to believe?

Yet another theory is that Oswald actually meant to kill Governor Connally. Connally had approved Oswald's dishonorable discharge from the military and refused to overturn it. Maybe Oswald wasn't an expert sniper who hit his target, the president, twice. He had been a decent shot in the military, but not an excellent one, and he'd already missed his target in an earlier assassination attempt of a military figure. Maybe he took advantage of the parade to try to get revenge on Connally and hit the president instead.

Regardless of the reasons behind Kennedy's assassination, the 1960s were a violent decade, with many protests against the government and the Vietnam War.

These years also saw several more high-profile assassinations. Kennedy's brother Robert Kennedy was murdered while running for president in the 1968 elections. Civil Rights leaders Malcolm X and Martin Luther King, Jr. were shot by assassins in 1965 and 1968. This has led many to wonder if the violence was the product of an angry and tumultuous decade or if some person or group was behind these terrible acts.

Activists Martin Luther King, Jr. (left) and Malcolm X (right) came to Washington, D.C., to see the Civil Rights Act signed into law in 1964. By the end of the decade, they would both be killed. Image courtesy of Wikimedia.

The 1960s also saw great steps forward. The Civil Rights Act of 1964 was passed largely in honor of Kennedy's memory. This law protected the rights of Black Americans and other non-White Americans against segregation and discrimination. The Voting Rights Act of 1965 protected every adult citizen's right to vote. And in 1969, America became the first nation to land a person on the moon, fulfilling another of Kennedy's goals.

As Kennedy himself said, "A man may die, nations may rise and fall, but an idea lives on."

Kennedy's official presidential portrait was painted after his assassination and reflects his tragic end. Image courtesy of Wikimedia.

EPILOGUE: A TANGLE OF TRIANGLES

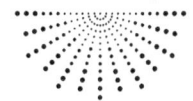

Bermuda. Bridgewater. Bennington. These famous "triangles" in the United States have long been known for strange occurrences and disappearances. People go missing, eerie shapes scuttle through the shadows, and technology glitches out. Are there hot spots of paranormal activity in the United States—places where strange things happen—or are these stories just coincidences?

The Bermuda Triangle is the most famous of these mysterious places. It extends across part of the Atlantic Ocean from roughly the bottom of Florida along the edge of the Caribbean to the US territory of Puerto Rico, and then out to the British island of Bermuda in the Atlantic Ocean about 700 miles from North Carolina. It's notorious for the number of ships and planes that have gone missing in its region. Some of these have simply vanished, while others have left strange clues behind.

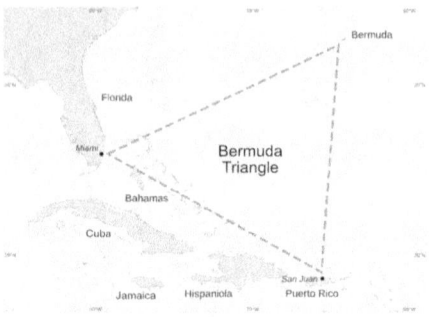

The Bermuda Triangle is located in dangerous waters.
Image courtesy of Wikimedia.

For instance, in 1918, the US Navy's *USS Cyclops* disappeared without a trace. It never sent out a distress call, and no sign of the ship or its 309-man crew was ever found. This occurred during World War I, when the *Cyclops* had been delivering coal for fuel to other ships. On its last journey, the *Cyclops* had been supporting British ships stationed off Brazil. It was returning to the United States with Brazilian ore for steel manufacturing. The Captain, George Worley, reported problems with one of the engines when preparing to leave Brazil, and he believed that the ship was loaded too heavily with ore, but he was ordered back to the US. The ship stopped once at the Caribbean island of Barbados because it was riding low in the water, but its load of ore was still secure, so it continued on, never to be seen again.

Without finding any wreckage of the ship, we may never know what happened to it and the hundreds of sailors on board. Some people think one of the German submarines patrolling the Caribbean sank the *Cyclops*, but the Germans have no record of an encounter with the ship. Others think the ship encountered a storm or a rogue wave. Because the ship was riding low in the water, it might have been easily tipped and sunk. Its sister ships, those built on the same plans, were later found to have structural weaknesses, so it could have snapped in half in particularly unlucky weather.

The USS Cyclops *before it vanished. Photo courtesy of the New York Navy Yard and Wikimedia.*

Other people point fingers at Captain George Worley. The US Navy discovered that he was actually Johan Frederick Wichmann, a German, and he had snuck off a ship into San Francisco in 1878. He maintained a strong loyalty to Germany, as did many of the men he hired. He had been accused of smuggling drugs with his private boat before he joined the US Navy. The men who sailed with him reported he had a terrible temper and erratic behavior, such as wandering the ship in only his underwear and a derby hat. Knowing this about him, people wonder if he tried to defect to Germany, or if he did something so bizarre that his men mutinied and somehow sank the ship. Still, there was never a distress call, so whatever happened, it happened fast.

In the following years, two sister ships of the *Cyclops*, *Proteus* and *Nereus* also disappeared without a trace in the

Bermuda Triangle. This time it was during World War II. Were all these ships casualties of war? Did the rough weather in the Bermuda Triangle doom the ships' weak structure? Or was some sinister force at play?

Ships went missing in the Bermuda Triangle outside of wartime as well. In 1967, a Florida man named Dan Burack sailed with a friend off the Florida coast in his yacht, *Witchcraft*, to look at Christmas lights in Miami. It was a clear December night, good for sailing. But at about 9 pm, Burack called the Coast Guard to say that his propeller had struck something in the water, damaging his boat, and he would need to be towed back to shore. The Coast Guard arrived 19 minutes later, but there was no sign of the *Witchcraft* or its passengers. The ship had vanished. A massive search effort scoured both above and below the ocean and along the coast, but no sign of the ship or its two passengers ever emerged. We also don't know what struck its propeller and damaged it.

Perhaps the most famous disappearance in the Bermuda Triangle is Flight 19. This was a US Navy pilot training flight that set out from Fort Lauderdale, Florida in the afternoon of December 5, 1945, soon after the end of World War II. There were fourteen men aboard 5 TMB Avenger bombers. They flew the first part of the training mission apparently without a problem, but then their messages became odd.

According to the U.S. Naval Institute, one of the student pilots said, "I don't know where we are. We must have gotten lost after that last turn."

Their instructor said, "Both my compasses are out, and I am trying to find Fort Lauderdale, Florida."

The base tried to send them instructions, but the planes either didn't hear or couldn't respond. The pilots remained confused about their location.

One of the students said, "...if we could just fly west we would get home..."

But the instructor thought they were already too far west of Florida and instructed them to fly east.

It was getting dark, and the weather turned stormy. A few radio transmitters in Florida picked up the planes' messages—coming from east of Florida. The last bits of conversation from the planes tell us that they were running low on gas and planning to ditch, or land together, on the choppy sea if they couldn't find a place to land.

The Navy sent out a huge search and rescue mission to either find the planes before they went down or find the men in the sea. Of course, even the pilots didn't know where they were, and the Navy wasn't sure where their planes had gone down.

Grumman TBF Avengers like the planes lost with Flight 19.
Image courtesy of the US Navy and Wikimedia.

Disaster—or the bad luck of the Bermuda Triangle—

wasn't finished with the US Navy that night. One of the rescue planes suddenly lost contact about twenty minutes into the rescue effort. A civilian ship in the area reported seeing a fireball in the sky and an oil slick on the water in the area where the rescue plane vanished. Something went terribly wrong with the rescue plane, but we may never know exactly what.

The pilots and planes from Flight 19 have never been recovered, despite a huge search effort at the time and ongoing interest ever since.

Some people believe that the Bermuda Triangle is cursed or home to strange energies or creatures that sometimes attack those who pass through it. Others point out that it's a huge section of ocean—larger than most countries—with deep trenches and dangerous weather. It was also once on the Agonic Line, a place where true north and magnetic north cross each other. True north is the actual North Pole of the globe, while magnetic north is a northern point created by the Earth's rotation and its shifting magnetic field. When the two line up, it makes it more difficult to read compasses correctly. This might have made it harder to navigate through the Bermuda Triangle (because the Earth's magnetic field shifts, this line is now further west, and modern navigation techniques easily account for it).

Statistically, the number of vessels that go missing in the Bermuda Triangle isn't unusually high compared to how large the area is. But that would be little comfort to the crew of the *Cyclops*, the *Witchcraft*, or Flight 19.

———

Though less famous than the Bermuda Triangle, the Bridgewater Triangle in Massachusetts also has a long history of strange occurrences. This "triangle" is centered around the Hockomock Swamp.

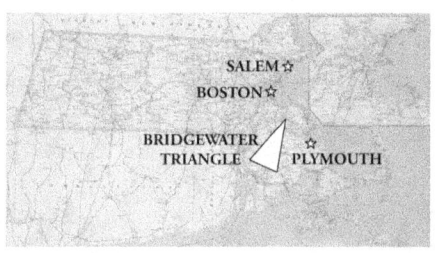

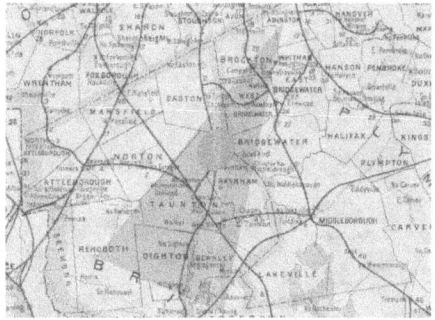

The top map shows the Bridgewater Triangle's location in Massachusetts, and the bottom map shows the location of Hockomock Swamp in the triangle. Based on a map from the Boston Public Library and Wikimedia.

Hockomock Swamp was the traditional burial ground of the Wampanoag people, who called it the "place of spirits." They believed it was home to Pukwudgies, or "Wild Men of the Woods." These were said to be small, hairy human-like creatures that were once friendly but turned vicious toward humans when the Wampanoag fought with them.

The Bridgewater Triangle is also home to the mysterious Dighton Rock. This large stone, first noted in writings by settlers in 1680, is covered with petroglyphs that don't belong to any known culture. Native American art experts have said it doesn't look like their symbols or petroglyphs. Some people think it's a remnant from Viking explorers who reached the Americas a thousand years ago, though it doesn't match their rune system either. It seems to belong to some unknown group that once lived in or visited the area and has since vanished.

The Dighton Rock. Image courtesy of Frank S. Davis and Wikimedia.

Once Europeans settled in the Bridgewater area, the Wampanoag's "place of the spirits" witnessed more deaths. In 1675-1676, colonists and the Wampanoag engaged in the bloodiest war in American history, called King Philip's War. About twenty-five percent of European settlers in America were killed, and up to eighty percent of the Wampanoag died or were sold into slavery. For comparison, the Civil War, which saw the highest number of deaths in an American war with over 600,000 killed, wiped out "only" 2 percent of the

American population. Much of the fighting of King Philip's War took place in the Bridgewater Triangle.

A nineteenth-century drawing imagining the fighting in King Philip's War. Image courtesy of Wikimedia.

There have been tragedies in more recent times, too. Taunton State Hospital is a deserted building in the Bridgewater Triangle with an eerie—some say haunted—vibe. A hospital might not sound like such a bad place, but when it opened in 1854, it was the State Lunatic Hospital at Taunton. It was designed to have more sunshine and fresh air than older mental asylums, but it still turned into a terrible place.

Many people think Taunton State Hospital is haunted. Image courtesy of Pictures Now and Alamy.

People with mental disabilities and mental health disorders were locked up at Taunton and other mental asylums alongside murderers. People could also be forced into the hospital if their family thought they were too loud or obnoxious or if they did things their family didn't like. Patients in nineteenth-century mental asylums were cut off from the world, crowded together in filthy rooms, bathed by having icy cold buckets of water dumped over them, fed gruel and rotten meat, surrounded by rats, and beaten by the staff if they complained. The Taunton Hospital was finally closed due to its inhumane conditions. Is it any wonder the empty buildings give people a bad feeling?

Nellie Bly was a daring young journalist who pretended to be insane so she could be locked in an asylum and tell us what really went on in these "hospitals." Image courtesy of the Library of Congress.

Some people believe ghosts linger at Taunton Hospital, and it's not the only supposedly haunted place in the Bridgewater Triangle. A red-headed hitchhiking ghost is said to linger along the highway that cuts through the area. According to local lore, the ghost vanishes when people pull over to pick him up or when he gets inside their car, leaving them with goosebumps and no explanation for what they've seen.

Strange lights also appear in the air in the Bridgewater Triangle. Reports of these lights go back to colonial times, if not earlier. Skeptics say it's only swamp gas—methane from decomposing matter in the Hockomock Swamp that floats free and ignites in the air. Others say the lights are ghosts, UFOs, or somehow connected to sightings of Bigfoot or the legendary Native American creature known as a thunderbird.

Whatever the truth, the Bridgewater Triangle has gathered a lot of mystery and tragedy over its history. Do you think places are affected by the terrible things that happen in them?

––––––

The mysteries of the Bermuda and Bridgewater triangles are spaced out over many years. The Bennington Triangle, on the other hand, is focused mainly on five strange disappearances between 1945 and 1950. This triangle is centered around Glastenbury Mountain in Vermont.

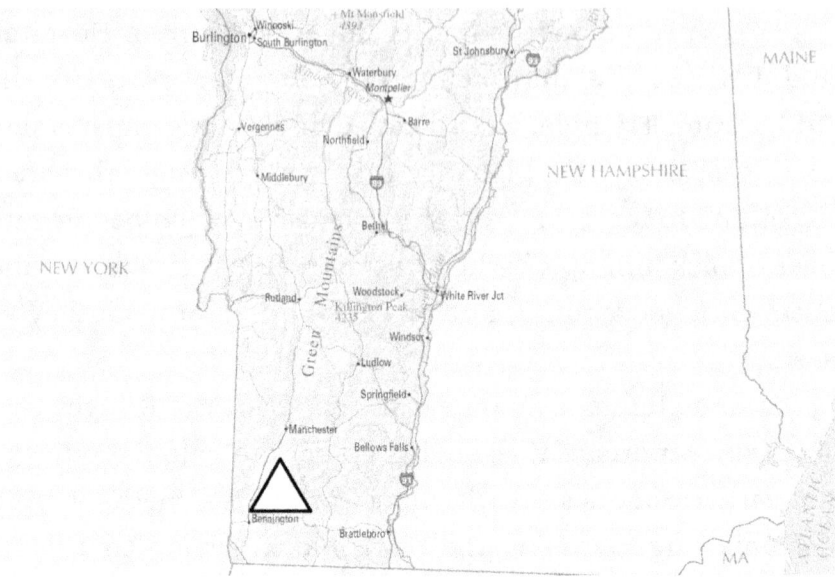

Glastenbury Mountain is just north of Bennington, Vermont. Image based on a map by the National Atlas.

The first of the Bennington Five to disappear was a hunting guide named Middie Rivers in 1945. The 74-year-old was leading some friends on a hunting expedition. He walked ahead of the group, and they lost sight of him. When they got to camp, there was no sign of Rivers. They couldn't find him and called out a search party of several hundred people. No sign of him has ever been found.

The next year, 18-year-old college student Paula Welden decided to walk the popular Long Trail at Glastenbury Mountain. Several witnesses saw her leave on her hike. When she didn't return the next day, over a thousand people, including some in airplanes, searched for her. Like Rivers, she had vanished without a trace.

Paula Jean Welden from her missing poster. Image courtesy of The Charley Project and Wikimedia.

Bennington had a few years' respite from disappearances. Then, in 1949, war veteran James Tedford vanished, apparently right off the bus going through Bennington. He was headed back to the veterans' home where he lived after visiting family. A friend saw him on the bus, but when they reached Tedford's stop, there was no sign of him.

The year 1950 rounded out the disappearances. First, eight-year-old Paul Jepson vanished when his parents left him alone for a short time. Bloodhounds traced his scent to the road, and from there it was gone.

Just over two weeks later, 53-year-old Frieda Langer was hiking with some family members. Her clothes got wet in a stream, so she went back to their campsite to change. Langer was never seen alive again. Unlike the others, searchers eventually found her body—almost a year later—in a local reservoir. No one knows how she died or how she ended up in the reservoir.

Some people have suspected that such a cluster of

disappearances might be the work of a human killer, and it's possible. The victims have nothing in common, though, except that they lived in the area. The Bennington Triangle is a large and dangerous section of wilderness. There are steep drop-offs, sudden storms, and freezing temperatures in the fall and winter, when most of the disappearances occurred. If someone became lost, they would be almost impossible to find in the rugged terrain and forested landscape. And once they had died, their body would be easily hidden by fallen leaves and branches. Many say these tragic losses are an unfortunate coincidence.

Another death just a few years before the main five, occurring in 1943, adds another twist to the story. In 1943, local hunter Carol Herrick vanished during a hunting trip. Searchers found his body several days later. Large footprints surrounded him, and it appeared that he had been crushed to death; his ribcage was broken, though the rest of his body showed little trauma.

Carol Herrick's death reminds some of an old story from the abandoned town of Glastenbury up the mountain. At one time in the late 1800s, a stagecoach was on its way up to visit the little town. The stagecoach stopped at a stream, and the horses began acting nervous. The driver hopped down and noticed huge footprints in the mud. Then, something large and hairy shoved the stagecoach, terrifying all the passengers, as well as the horses, and almost tipping the stagecoach. The attacker then ran away. That led to rumors about a wild man living in the woods, perhaps a crazed killer. Of course, modern people immediately think of Bigfoot.

———

Debate about these triangles is likely to continue as long as people are interested in their stories. Whether you believe the strange events are natural or supernatural is up to you. But it's good to remember that America is a huge country with vast wilderness areas that have only barely been explored or mapped. It's the fourth-largest country in the world, by area, after Russia, Canada, and China. Despite all of our modern technology, there are places we hardly know about, and people go missing in the wilderness every year. In fact, these are only three of the many places in the United States that have a long history of strange stories and legends. So, if you go searching for mysteries in this vast landscape, be prepared and don't hike alone.

SELECTED SOURCES AND FURTHER READING

Disclaimer: The author and publisher provide these links for informational purposes only and do not endorse or control the content of any resources listed below. Hyperlinks may become out of date and some sources may contain ads or information that is inaccurate, outdated, or sensitive. The author and publisher assume no responsibility or liability for the content of outside sources.

Montezuma's Gold

Lynn Blamires, "ATV Adventures: A tale of Montezuma's lost gold in Three Lakes Canyon near Kanab," Standard-Examiner, December 28, 2023. https://www.standard.net/lifestyle/recreation/2023/dec/28/atv-adventures-a-tale-of-montezumas-lost-gold-in-three-lakes-canyon-near-kanab/

Cortés on La Noche Triste or The Night of Sorrows, American Historical Association Resource Library, https://www.historians.org/resource/cortes-on-la-noche-triste-or-the-night-of-sorrows/

The Memoirs of the Conquistador Bernal Diaz del Castillo, Vol 1 (of 2) Written by Himself Containing a True and Full Account of the Discovery and Conquest of Mexico and New Spain. Translator: John Ingram Lockhart Project Gutenberg, https://www.gutenberg.org/files/32474/32474-h/32474-h.htm#CHAPTER_CXXVI

Dumbarton Oaks Museum, Snail Shell Ornaments, March 8, 2023, https://museum.doaks.org/objects-1/info/22596

Encyclopedia Britannica, "Aztec," https://www.britannica.com/topic/Aztec

Jackson Foster, The History of the Aztecs on their Terms: A Q&A with NEH Public Scholar Camilla Townsend, October 28, 2020, National Endowment for the Humanities Blog, https://www.neh.gov/blog/history-aztecs-their-terms-qa-neh-public-scholar-camilla-townsend

Hal Johnson, Magic of Kanab Podcast, Transcript at Kane County Office of Tourism and Film Commission, "Treasure Hunting in Southern Utah with Dan Dillman."

Kane County Office of Tourism and Film Commission, "The Wild 100+ Year Search for Montezuma's Treasure in Kanab, Utah." https://visitsouthernutah.com/blog/the-wild-100-year-search-for-montezumas-treasure-in-kanab-utah/

Lee Edward Littler, The Mesoamerican Connection: Central American diffusion into the North American Southwest, Mexicolore, May 13, 2018 https://www.mexicolore.co.uk/aztecs/you-contribute/mesoamerica-and-the-north-american-southwest

Theresa Machemer, "Spanish Conquistadors Stole This Gold Bar From Aztec Emperor Moctezuma's Trove," January 14, 2020, Smithsonian Magazine, https://www.smithsonianmag.com/smart-news/gold-bar-once-belonged-aztec-emperor-moctezuma-180973959/

Tasmin Mahfuz, "Montezuma's Gold: Is there cursed Aztec Gold in Utah?" ABC4 News, February 6, 2015, https://www.abc4.com/news/montezumas-gold-is-there-cursed-aztec-gold-in-utah/

Alyson M. Thibodeau, et al, "Was Aztec and Mixtec turquoise mined in the American Southwest?" *Science Advances* 13 Jun 2018 Vol 4, Issue 6, https://www.science.org/doi/10.1126/sciadv.aas9370

The Lost Colony

Kelly Agan and T. Mike Childs, "The Dare Stones," NCpedia, SLNC Government & Heritage Library, 2019, https://www.ncpedia.org/dare-stones

Livia Gershon, "Pottery Fragments May Hold Clues to Roanoke Colonists' Fate," Smithsonian Magazine, November 9, 2020.

Kristina Killgrove, "'Lost Colony' of Roanoke may have assimilated into Indigenous society, archaeologist claims — but not everyone is convinced," Live Science, June 10, 2025, https://www.livescience.com/archaeology/lost-colony-of-roanoke-may-have-assimilated-into-indigenous-society-archaeologist-claims-but-not-everyone-is-convinced

John White, "John White's Attempts to Rescue the Roanoke Colonists," National Humanities Center, https://nationalhumanitiescenter.org/pds/amerbegin/exploration/text6/white.pdf

John White, The Fifth Voyage of John M. White, 1590, American Journeys Collections, Wisconsin Historical Society Digital Library and Archives, https://www.americanjourneys.org/AJ_PDF/AJ-038.pdf

John White, The Fourth Voyage Made to Virginia, in the Yere 1587, American Journeys Collections, Wisconsin Historical Society Digital Library and Archives, https://content.wisconsinhistory.org/digital/collection/aj/id/2360

Witch Hunt

Lindsey Berebitsky, "Could a fungus be behind the Salem witch trials?" Purdue University College of Agriculture College News, October 24, 2024, https://ag.purdue.edu/news/2024/10/could-a-fungus-be-behind-the-salem-witch-trials.html

Erin Blakemore, "Women Weren't the Only Victims of the Salem Witch Trials," History.com, October 13, 2017, https://www.history.com/articles/women-werent-only-victims-of-salem-witch-trials

Jess Blumberg, "A Brief History of the Salem Witch Trials," Smithsonian Magazine, October 23, 2007, updated October 24, 2022, https://www.

smithsonianmag.com/history/a-brief-history-of-the-salem-witch-trials-175162489/

Rebecca Beatrice Brooks, "The Witchcraft Trial of Mary Warren," History of Massachusetts Blog, August 13, 2013, https://historyofmassachusetts.org/mary-warren/

John Hale, "A modest enquiry into the nature of witchcraft" [1697], Evans Early American Imprint Collection, University of Michigan Library Digital Collections, https://quod.lib.umich.edu/cgi/t/text/text-idx?c=evans;cc=evans;rgn=main;view=text;idno=N00872.0001.001

Deodat Lawson, "A Brief and True Narrative, 1692," University of Virginia Library, https://xtf.lib.virginia.edu/xtf/view?docId=modern_english/uvaGenText/tei/BurNarr.xml;chunk.id=d7;toc.depth=1;toc.id=d7;brand=default

Matt Madden, "Examination of Rebecca Nurse of Salem Village," Salem Witch Trials Documentary Archive and Transcript Project, University of Virginia, 2001, https://salem.lib.virginia.edu/people/nursecourt.html

Jules Montague, "Can an auto-immune illness explain the Salem witch trials?" BBC, January 2, 2019, https://www.bbc.com/future/article/20181221-can-an-auto-immune-illness-explain-the-salem-witch-trials

Salem Witch Museum, "Border Disputes," https://salemwitchmuseum.com/locations/border-disputes/

Vicki Saxon, "What Caused the Salem Witch Trials?" JSTOR Daily, October 27, 2015, https://daily.jstor.org/caused-salem-witch-trials/

Laura Wolff Scanlan, "The Salem Witch Trials According to the Historical Records," HUMANITIES, Winter 2022, Volume 43, Number 1, https://www.neh.gov/article/records-salem-witch-trials

The Pirate's Missing Loot

Isis Davis-Marks, "17th-Century Coins Found in a Fruit Grove May Solve a 300-Year-Old Pirate Mystery," *Smithsonian Magazine*, April 12, 2021, https://www.smithsonianmag.com/smart-news/17th-century-coins-found-fruit-grove-solve-pirate-mystery-180977401/

Captain Charles Johnson, *A General History of the Pyrates*, London, 1724, available at Project Gutenberg, https://www.gutenberg.org/files/40580/40580-h/40580-h.htm#page-84

Andrew Lawler, "Three Centuries after His Beheading, a Kinder, Gentler Blackbeard Emerges," *Smithsonian Magazine*, November 13, 2018. https://www.smithsonianmag.com/history/three-centuries-after-his-beheading-kinder-gentler-blackbeard-emerges-180970782/

Robert E. Lee "Blackbeard the Pirate ." NCpedia, State Library of NC, 1986. https://www.ncpedia.org/biography/blackbeard-the-pirate

National Park Service staff, "Blackbeard (Edward Teach)," Cape Hatteras National Seashore, September 27, 2021, https://www.nps.gov/caha/learn/historyculture/blackbeard-edward-teach.htm

Queen Anne's Revenge Project, "Artifacts from Queen Anne's Revenge," https://www.qaronline.org/conservation/artifacts

Abigail Tucker, "Did Archeologists Uncover Blackbeard's Treasure?" *Smithsonian Magazine*, March 2011, https://www.smithsonianmag.com/history/did-archaeologists-uncover-blackbeards-treasure-215890/

A Lady Spy

Claire Bellerjeau and Tiffany Yecke Brooks, "Did an Enslaved Woman Try to Warn the Americans of Benedict Arnold's Treason?" *Smithsonian Magazine*, May 16, 2022. https://www.smithsonianmag.com/history/did-an-enslaved-woman-try-to-warn-the-americans-of-benedict-arnolds-treason-180980080/?itm_source=parsely-api

Claire Bellerjeau and Tiffany Yecke Brooks, "Finding Liss," *New York Archives Magazine*, Fall 2022.

Bill Bleyer, "George Washington's Culper Spy Ring: Separating Fact from Fiction," *Journal of the American Revolution*, June 3, 2021, https://allthingsliberty.com/2021/06/george-washingtons-culper-spy-ring-separating-fact-from-fiction/

Bill Bleyer, "The Myth of Agent 355," Women Who Shaped History, Smithsonian Magazine, March 21, 2022, https://www.smithsonianmag.com/history/the-myth-of-agent-355-the-woman-spy-who-supposedly-helped-win-the-revolutionary-war-180979748/

Elizabeth Burgin, Letter to James Caldwell, November 19, 1779, https://founders.archives.gov/documents/Washington/03-23-02-0550-0002

Don N. Hagist, "Elizabeth Burgin Helps the Prisoners... Somehow" *Journal of the American Revolution*, September 11, 2014, https://allthingsliberty.com/2014/09/elizabeth-burgin-helps-the-prisoners-somehow/

History.com editors, "The Culper Spy Ring," History.com, February 27, 2025, https://www.history.com/articles/culper-spy-ring

Jake Kerridge, "The mystery of Agent 355, America's first female spy," *The Telegraph*, January 11, 2022, https://www.telegraph.co.uk/films/0/americas-first-female-spy-mystery-agent-355/

Michael Schellhammer, "Abraham Woodhull: The Spy Named Samuel Culper," *Journal of the American Revolution*, May 19, 2014. https://allthingsliberty.com/2014/05/abraham-woodhull-the-spy-named-samuel-culper/

John L. Smith, Jr., 9 Rules of Spying that Nathan Hale Failed to Follow," *Journal of the American Revolution*, May 21, 2015, https://allthingsliberty.com/2015/05/9-rules-of-spying-that-nathan-hale-failed-to-follow/#_edn17

Mark Sternburg: "Selah Strong: Records Reveal an Overlooked Hero of the Culper Spy Ring," *New York Archives Magazine*, Fall 2022.

George Washington, Letter to Samuel Huntington, 25 December 1779, https://founders.archives.gov/documents/Washington/03-23-02-0550-0001-0001

Kathryn White, "Benjamin Tallmadge," Washington Library: Center for Digital History, Mount Vernon, https://www.mountvernon.org/library/digitalhistory/digital-encyclopedia/article/benjamin-tallmadge

The Vanished Explorer

Lewis & Clark National Historic Trail, "York After the Expedition," National Park Service, https://www.nps.gov/articles/000/york-after-the-expedition.htm

Shoshi Parks, "York Explored the West With Lewis and Clark, but His Freedom Wouldn't Come Until Decades Later," *Smithsonian Magazine*, March 8, 2018, https://www.smithsonianmag.com/history/york-explored-west-lewis-and-clark-his-freedom-wouldnt-come-until-decades-later-180968427/

Darrell M. Millner, "York of the Corps of Discovery," *Oregon Historical Quarterly*, 2003, https://www.ohs.org/oregon-historical-quarterly/upload/104_3_Millner_York.pdf

Joseph A. Mussulman, "York in the Journals," Lewis and Clark Trail Alliance, https://lewis-clark.org/people/york/york-in-journals/

Oregon Treasure Hunt

John Wesley Hillman, Hillman Memoirs, in Southern Oregon History revised, 1915, revised April 24, 2025, https://truwe.sohs.org/files/hillman2.html

Finn J.D. John, "Offbeat Oregon: Oregon's wildest lost-cabin gold mine story may be true... or not," *Lincoln County Leader*, May 4, 2020, https://www.thenewsguard.com/community_paid/offbeat-oregon-oregon-s-wildest-lost-cabin-gold-mine-story-may-be-true-or-not/article_87dea6ae-8e51-11ea-ad21-5b21d168dac5.html

Finn J.D. John, "Quest for lost gold mine led to 12,000-acre jewel," *Offbeat Oregon*, July 8, 2012, https://www.offbeatoregon.com/1207b-crater-lake-discovered-by-legendary-gold-mine-seekers.html

H. John Runkel, "Crater Lake Discovery Centennial," *Crater Lake National Park Nature Notes*, 1953, https://npshistory.com/nature_notes/crla/vol19b.htm

Lyn Topinka, "Discovery of Crater Lake, Oregon, June 12, 1852, United States Geological Survey, https://volcanoes.usgs.gov/observatories/cvo/Historical/discovery_crater_lake_1853.shtml

Danger in the Water

Friends of the Hunley, "The H.L. Hunley's Sinkings," https://www.hunley.org/the-hunleys-sinkings/

Friends of the Hunley, "The Evidence," https://www.hunley.org/the-evidence/

Rachel Lance, "The New Explosive Theory About What Doomed the Crew of the 'Hunley,'" *Smithsonian Magazine*, March 2020, https://www.smithsonianmag.com/history/new-explosive-theory-what-doomed-crew-hunley-180974159/

Christopher D. Rucker, "The Myth of the Hunley's Blue Lantern," *The Civil War Monitor*, October 8, 2012, https://www.civilwarmonitor.com/the-myth-of-the-h-l-hunleys-blue-lantern/

Tut Underwood, "Disappearance of the Hunley Remains a Mystery 158 Years Later," South Carolina Public Radio, https://www.southcarolina

publicradio.org/sc-news/2022-03-25/disappearance-of-the-hunley-remains-a-mystery-158-years-later

US Navy, "The Sinking of the USS *Housatonic* by the Submarine CSS *H.L. Hunley*, off Charleston, South Carolina, 17 February 1864: Original US Navy Documents," Naval History and Heritage Command, https://www.history.navy.mil/research/library/online-reading-room/title-list-alphabetically/s/the-sinking-of-the-uss-housatonic-by-the-submarine-css-h-l-hunley.html

The Greenbriar Ghost

Belinda Anderson, "Greenbriar Ghost, Zona Heaster Shue," Experience Greenbriar Valley, https://greenbrierwv.com/editorials/the-greenbrier-ghost

Jennifer Jones, "Death did not silence her: The Murder of Zona Heaster Shue," The Dead History, April 22, 2025, https://thedeadhistory.com/2025/04/22/zona-heaster-shue/

Joey Rather, "How 'The Greenbriar Ghost' helped convict a West Virginia murderer in 1897," Paranormal W.Va., 12WBOY News, January 23, 2023, https://www.wboy.com/only-on-wboy-com/paranormal-w-va/how-the-greenbrier-ghost-helped-convict-a-west-virginia-murderer-in-1897/

West Virginia Archives and History, "The Greenbriar Ghost," West Virginia Department of Arts, Culture, and History, Various June and July 1897 dated newspaper clippings, https://archive.wvculture.org/history/crime/shuearticles.html

The Trial of Joe Hill

Bureau of Labor Statistics, "History of child labor in the United States—part one: little children working," Monthly Labor Review, January 2017, https://www.bls.gov/opub/mlr/2017/article/history-of-child-labor-in-the-united-states-part-1.htm

Jonathan Grossman, "Fair Labor Standards Act of 1938: Maximum Struggle for a Minimum Wage," US Department of Labor, https://www.dol.gov/general/aboutdol/history/flsa1938

Jeremy Harmon, "Joe Hill: The Making of a Martyr," *Salt Lake Tribune*, https://local.sltrib.com/charts/joehill/hill.html

Sheila R. McCann, "The Trial of Joe Hill," *Salt Lake Tribune*, https://local.sltrib.com/charts/joehill/trial.html

Ogden Daily Standard, "Cartoon Found in Applequist Room," January 20, 1914, https://newspapers.lib.utah.edu/details?id=6735230

Salt Lake Tribune, "Governor Will Offer Reward for Murderers," January 12, 1914, https://newspapers.lib.utah.edu/details?id=14484559

The Gangster's Secret

Kathy Alexander, "Mobster Dutch Schultz & His Hidden Treasure," Legends of America, January 2024, https://www.legendsofamerica.com/dutch-schultz/

Biography.com Editors, "Dutch Schultz," August 10, 2020, https://www.biography.com/crime/dutch-schultz

Cloey Callahan, "A modern-day scavenger hunt for an old mobster's money," *Times-Union*, July 20, 2021, https://www.timesunion.com/hudsonvalley/news/article/modern-hunt-for-dutch-schultz-treasure-catskills-16317319.php

Valerie Edwards, "New documentary follows treasure hunters hunting gangster's loot," *The Daily Mail*, November 15, 2020, https://www.dailymail.co.uk/news/article-8950857/New-documentary-follows-treasure-hunters-hunting-gangsters-loot.html

Dutch Schultz, "The Last Words of Dutch Schultz," Internet Archive

Wayback Machine, https://web.archive.org/web/20070607184913/http://www.feastofhateandfear.com/archives/dutch.html

Mary Witkowski, "Dutch Schultz," Bridgeport History Center, Bridgeport Library (Connecticut), https://bportlibrary.org/hc/heroes-and-villains/dutch-schultz/

The Ghost Blimp of World War II

Andrew Chamings and Katie Dowd, "In 1942, a war blimp fell out of the sky onto Daly City. Its crew was never found," SFGate, November 19, 2020, https://www.sfgate.com/sfhistory/article/SF-Ghost-blimp-Daly-City-15739903.php

"Crewless Blimp Crashes in Strange Mystery Case," *Imperial Valley Press*, August 17, 1942, page 6, https://chroniclingamerica.loc.gov/lccn/sn92070146/1942-08-17/ed-1/seq-6/#date1=1777&index=1&rows=20&words=Cody+DeWitt+Ernest&searchType=basic&sequence=0&state=&date2=1963&proxtext=%22ernest+dewitt+cody%22&y=0&x=0&dateFilterType=yearRange&page=1

"Crewless Blimp Mystery Deepens," *Imperial Valley Press*, August 18, 1942, page 6, https://chroniclingamerica.loc.gov/lccn/sn92070146/1942-08-18/ed-1/seq-6/#date1=1777&index=2&rows=20&words=Hill+James+Riley&searchType=basic&sequence=0&state=&date2=1963&proxtext=%22james+riley+hill%22&y=0&x=0&dateFilterType=yearRange&page=1

Greg Daugherty, "The 80-Year Mystery of the U.S. Navy's 'Ghost Blimp,'" Smithsonian Magazine, August 16, 2022, https://www.smithsonianmag.com/history/the-80-year-mystery-of-the-us-navys-ghost-blimp-180980531/

John J. Geoghegan, "A Navy Blimp Took Off on a Routine Patrol Off the Coast. Its Crew Would Never Be Seen Again." Historynet, April 12, 2016, https://www.historynet.com/ghost-blimp-mystery-1-8/

Irwin Ross, "The Mystery of the L-8," U.S. Naval Institute Proceedings, March 1970, https://www.usni.org/magazines/proceedings/1970/march/mystery-l-8

Samantha Thomas, "Ghost Blimp," *Plane & Pilot*, March 3, 2021, https://www.planeandpilotmag.com/news/2021/03/03/ghost-blimp/

USNA Virtual Memorial Hall, "Ernest D. Cody, Lt, USN," https://usnamemorialhall.org/index.php/ERNEST_D._CODY,_LT,_USN

US Navy, "The Riddle of the L-8," Fleet Airships Atlantic Intelligence Bulletin Number 2, 8 August 1943, National Air and Space Museum Archives, https://edan.si.edu/slideshow/viewer/?eadrefid=NASM.1994.0022_ref119

The Death of a President

ABC News, "Jacqueline Kennedy Reveals That JFK Feared an LBJ Presidency," September 8, 2011," https://abcnews.go.com/Politics/Jacqueline_Kennedy/jacqueline-kennedy-reveals-jfk-feared-lbj-presidency/story?id=14477930

Owen Amos, "JFK assassination: Questions that won't go away," BBC News, October 24, 2017, https://www.bbc.com/news/world-us-canada-41741216

John Hanna and Jamie Stengle, "Newly released JFK assasination files reveal more about CIA but don't yet point to conspiracies," AP News, March 25, 2025, https://www.ap.org/news-highlights/spotlights/2025/newly-released-jfk-assassination-files-reveal-more-about-cia-but-dont-yet-point-to-conspiracies/

Arnold Kemp, "Forget JFK conspiracy, it was 'a mistake,'" September 19, 1999, https://www.theguardian.com/world/1999/sep/19/arnoldkemp.theobserver

John F. Kennedy Presidential Library and Museum, "Cuban Missile Crisis," https://www.jfklibrary.org/learn/about-jfk/jfk-in-history/cuban-missile-crisis

John F. Kennedy Presidential Library and Museum, "John F. Kennedy Quotations," https://www.jfklibrary.org/learn/about-jfk/life-of-john-f-kennedy/john-f-kennedy-quotations

John F. Kennedy Presidential Library and Museum, "The Modern Civil Rights Movement and the Kennedy Administration," https://www.jfklibrary.org/learn/about-jfk/jfk-in-history/civil-rights-movement

Alex Johnson, "JFK Files: J. Edgar Hoover Said Public Must Believe Lee Harvey Oswald Acted Alone," NBC News, October 27, 2017, https://www.nbcnews.com/storyline/jfk-assassination-files/jfk-files-j-edgar-hoover-said-public-must-believe-lee-n814881

Dr. Howard Markel, "John F. Kennedy kept these medical struggles private," November 22, 2019, PBS News, https://www.pbs.org/newshour/health/john-f-kennedy-kept-these-medical-struggles-private

President's Commission on the Assassination of President John F. Kennedy, "Warren Commission Report: Table of Contents," National Archives, https://www.archives.gov/research/jfk/warren-commission-report/toc

A Tangle of Triangles

Kathy Alexander, "Bennington Triangle, Vermont," Legends of America, October 2023, https://www.legendsofamerica.com/bennington-triangle-vermont/

Kathy Alexander, "Bridgewater Triangle, Massachusetts," Legends of America, May 2025, https://www.legendsofamerica.com/bridgewater-triangle-massachusetts/

Joe Bills, "The Mystery of Dighton Rock," New England.com, October 14, 2021, https://newengland.com/travel/massachusetts/the-mystery-of-dighton-rock/

Tim Newcomb, "A Scientist Says He's Solved the Bermuda Triangle, Just Like That," *Popular Mechanics*, August 9, 2025, https://www.popularmechanics.com/science/a65643514/is-bermuda-triangle-mystery-solved/

Breana Pitts, "It Happens Here: A look at the 'weirdness' of the Bridgewater Triangle," CBS WBZ News, October 27, 2022, https://www.cbsnews.com/boston/news/the-bridgewater-triangle-abington-rehoboth-massachusetts-wbz-tv-it-happens-here/

Ripley's Believe It or Not! "The Bennington Disappearances: Vermont's Very Own Bermuda Triangle," Lethbridge News Now, October 12, 2023, https://lethbridgenewsnow.com/2023/10/12/the-bennington-disappearances-vermonts-very-own-bermuda-triangle/

Tim Weisberg, "What Is Massachusetts' Bridgewater Triangle?" WBSM News, October 17, 2020, https://wbsm.com/what-is-massachusetts-bridgewater-triangle/

Howard Weiss-Tisman and Burgess Brown, "The Bennington Triangle: How 5 mysterious disappearances developed a cult following online," Brave Little State, March 6, 2025, https://www.vermontpublic.org/podcast/brave-little-state/2025-03-06/the-bennington-triangle-how-5-mysterious-disappearances-developed-a-cult-following-online

Frankie Witzenburg, "The Mysterious Disappearance of Flight 19," *Naval History*, U.S. Naval Institute, October 2021, https://www.usni.org/magazines/naval-history-magazine/2021/october/mysterious-disappearance-flight-19

ALSO BY E.B. WHEELER

British Fiction:

Born to Treason

The Royalist's Daughter

The Haunting of Springett Hall

Wishwood (Westwood Gothic)

Moon Hollow (Westwood Gothic)

A Proper Dragon (Dragons of Mayfair 1)

An Elusive Dragon (Dragons of Mayfair 2)

A Subtle Dragon (Dragons of Mayfair 3)

Cruel Magic (Iron & Thorns 1)

Wild Magic (Iron & Thorns 2)

Fierce Magic (Iron & Thorns 3)

A Haunted Masquerade (A Haunted Season)

Utah Fiction:

No Peace with the Dawn (with Jeffery Bateman)

Letters from the Homefront (Utah at War)

Balm for the Heart (Utah at War)

Bootleggers and Basil (in *The Pathways to the Heart*)

Blood in a Dry Town (Tenny Mateo Mystery 1)

A Company of Bones (Tenny Mateo Mystery 2)

Nonfiction:

Utah Women: Pioneers, Poets & Politicians

Mysteries of the Old West

Mysteries of the Middle Ages

Mysteries of the Modern World

Juvenile Fiction:

The Bone Map

Alejandra the Axolotl and the Big Mess

ACKNOWLEDGMENTS

Thank you to my critique group The Writers' Cache and to my beta readers, Alex, Dan, Karen, and Lael for their feedback and taking some of the mystery out of writing. And as always, I couldn't do this without the understanding, patience, and support of my family and especially my husband.

Links to Creative Commons image licenses:

GNU 2.5 (https://www.gnu.org/licenses/old-licenses/gpl-2.0.html)

CC BY 2.0 (https://creativecommons.org/licenses/by/2.0/)

CC BY-SA 2.0 (https://creativecommons.org/licenses/by-sa/2.0/)

CC BY-SA 3.0 (https://creativecommons.org/licenses/by-sa/3.0/)

CC BY 4.0 (https://creativecommons.org/licenses/by/4.0/)

CC BY-SA 4.0 (https://creativecommons.org/licenses/by-sa/4.0/)

ABOUT THE AUTHOR

E.B. Wheeler attended BYU, majoring in history with an English minor, and earned graduate degrees in history and landscape architecture from Utah State University. She's the author of over a dozen books, including *The Bone Map, Utah Women: Pioneers, Poets & Politicians,* and Whitney Award winner *Cruel Magic,* as well as several short stories, magazine articles, and scripts for educational programs. The League of Utah Writers named her the Writer of the Year in 2016. In addition to writing, she consults about historic preservation and teaches history.